Cultivating Genius

Cultivating Genius

The Why and How of Creating a 20% Time Learning Environment

Don Eckert

Copyright © 2016 Don Eckert
All rights reserved.

ISBN-13: 9780997307504
ISBN-10: 0997307501

Introduction

I began teaching in 1988, before schools had e-mail, laptops, cell phones and a host of other technology that we now take for granted. I have gone back to school several times, earning two Bachelor's Degrees and two Master's Degrees. I have spent countless hours in professional development sessions and have also pursued my passion of educational technology outside of the school setting. The culmination of my years of experience and education along with my partnership with Melissa Hellwig have led me to believe that schools need a revolution, not an evolution.

Melissa and I have been teaching partners at Hixson Middle School in Webster Groves, Missouri for ten years. Hixson is a traditional middle school that divides the kids into teams. Each team consists of about 100 students. There are three teams at each grade level, seventh and eighth, and one half team at each grade level. A half team consists of 50 students and two teachers (the two team teachers each teach two subjects). We teach on the school's seventh grade half team, Harmony Team. It is from our team name and our philosophy of learning that we coined the name Harmonized Learning. Our educational philosophies, and life philosophies for that matter, are in sync. Over the years, we have developed a rapport unparalleled in most school buildings. We know each other so well that if you're talking to only one of us, then you are really talking to both of us. Over the course of those ten years, we have developed a trust that is unbreakable. We have the utmost belief and faith in each other. We take risks together, we try new things in the classroom together, and we are always there to support each other.

One morning in late August, 2013, Melissa came in and said to me, "I watched a bunch of TED Talks last night. Have you ever heard of '20% Time'? I want to do it. I want to at least do it in my classes, but we could do it as a team."

"That's awesome! I'm in!" I said. "By the way, what's '20% Time'?"

Such is the nature of our relationship. If she was excited about "20% Time", then I knew it was something that would benefit both our kids as well as ourselves as teachers. Since we are of the same mind, I knew and trusted that she would have evaluated and analyzed the potential for the program and decided that it was worth doing. Sometimes, you have to throw the books out the window and try something completely cutting-edge. We had a new project.

So what is "20% Time"? "20% Time" is a way for teachers to allow students to pursue their own passions during the school day. Kids are learning all of the time. They are passionate about many things. They are sponges. The problem is that often we don't connect the classroom learning with the kids' interests. In a "20% Time" learning environment, teachers dedicate 20% of their class time so that students can pursue their own learning projects using any resources they have available to them. Google made "20% Time" famous when founders Larry Page and Sergey Brin encouraged employees to spend 20% of their work time pursuing passion projects, believing that the employees would invent things that would benefit Google. From these "20% Time" projects, Google News, Gmail and AdSense were developed. The goal of "20% Time" in our classes is to leverage students' natural curiosity and foster intrinsic motivation in the classroom.

Over the next month and a half, Melissa and I brainstormed, researched, collaborated and dreamt. We cobbled together the makings of a program outline, knowing that we would be throwing out a lot, keeping some and tweaking plenty. After all, no one gets it right the first time out of the box and everyone fails everyday. Those were lessons that we knew already and lessons that our kids would be learning big-time. We know that we learn the most when we fail and pick ourselves up and try again. We were comfortable with failure and learning from failure; now it was time to help the kids learn to "fail forward" and be comfortable with learning from that failure.

This book is a culmination of our work over the past several years. It is divided into two parts. In the first half, we talk about the philosophical underpinnings of "20% Time" as we see them and how our kiddos are no longer well-served by traditional schools and conventional methods of education. Those traditional methods prepared kids for an industrial manufacturing job, but now we as teachers and administrators are preparing kids for jobs and careers that don't even exist yet. How do you prepare a student for a world that hasn't even been imagined? That thought scares the bejeezus out of us. How can we possibly change schools to better serve kids? Using "20% Time", "Genius Hour", "FedEx Days", and similar programs is one way to help kids become lifelong learners.

The second half of the book is a template, if you will, for a "20% Time" program. It includes all of the documents that Melissa and I use along the way. Surely we don't expect other teachers to implement a "20% Time" program exactly as we do. Each teacher or group of teachers has their own set of circumstances, curricular and otherwise, and we realize that for the most part they must fit "20% Time" within those parameters. Our template is just that, a template. We want teachers to take from it what they want and reject what they don't want. We want them to use this book as a springboard to help spark their students' creativity, find the kiddos' inner geniuses, cultivate their students' passions, and come up with even better ideas to fit their unique situations. The template is a beginning-to-end, step-by-step process of how our "20% Time" grew from a conversation two teaching partners had before school one morning to a program that really works; a how-to guide, if you will.

The first part of the book is the "why". The second part of the book is the "how". We hope that, in its entirety, this book will give teachers, administrators, and other educators a rationale for trying this amazing way of enhancing their students' learning, while also offering practical, hands-on tools to help build a "20% Time" program tailored to any school, or non-school, situation. "20% Time" has been incredibly rewarding for our students and ourselves. We hope that everyone who reads this book finds their own program equally rewarding.

Part 1
Why schools must change to incorporate personalized learning like "20% Time".

"20% Time" is not about a class format or a process of learning. It is about opening up minds to the possibilities of school and life, not just the students' minds, but our own as well. It is about seeing the world around us and choosing to be actively engaged. It is about making the world a better place by creating solutions to problems that are the most immediate to us or that most interest us. "20% Time" is the way adults learn, even if we don't recognize it. It is the learning we do in our "spare time". It is the learning we want to do. "20% Time" is the learning of life, and the sooner we can introduce this kind of learning to the kids, the better off they, and we, will be.

Kids Are Different...or Are They?

We hear it all of the time: "Kids are different these days. Kids are not the same as they were when I started teaching." Well, that's true... and false. I started teaching in 1988. Education was different then. It was very traditional. Teachers were expected to lecture about the topic and kids were expected to listen attentively, copy notes and prepare eventually to take a test over the material. I must admit that I was a huge failure in this model.

Today we expect kids to move in class, to do things, to talk as well as listen, and to create. We communicate our goals for the kids and guide them in their learning. We do NOT blather on about our topic and expect kids to sit quietly copying notes for an eventual test. Well, most of us do not. Some still do. But the expectations around the classroom have changed dramatically in the past twenty five years. But have kids changed?

In the 1980's, the expectation was that kids would sit quietly listening to the teacher. While that was the expectation, it doesn't mean that the kids weren't bored stiff. They daydreamed, fidgeted, passed notes, and did just about anything to entertain themselves. Today, kids do the same thing when listening to wall-to-wall lecturing. Nothing has changed there, except that now instead of passing notes, they "Snapchat" their friends, check for Instagram updates, or game on their devices under their desks.

In the 1980's there was very little technology available in schools. We had access to a shared computer lab for writing but other than that, technology was scarce. The teacher was the most important person in the room. The teacher was expected to be the resident expert and the kids got everything from them, trickle-down style. Learning was not democratic. Learning was planned and carried out by the teacher. Students were just passive recipients of what the teacher thought was best for them.

Today, technology is much more universal. Kids bring phones, tablets, laptops and other technology items to school. Schools even provide technology to the students, like in our school's 1:1 Chromebook program, so that we can enhance learning. When teachers and students use this technology well, education is democratic. Kids become both learner and teacher. In this modern classroom, the teacher also assumes the role of both the giver and recipient of knowledge. We are able to develop a real community of learners. Teachers assume the role of facilitator. Kids can use what the teacher gives them as a springboard to other things that they may find more interesting.

Admittedly, some teachers not have evolved. They are clinging to the days of yore when the teacher was the focal point of the classroom. Believe me, I get it. Change is scary, and it is not always easy, but to preserve this type of classroom structure, the teacher must go against the evolution of schools as well as the needs of their students. While everyone else is moving forward by changing the structure of the classroom to include more technology, more learning, more active participation by students, and more personalization of learning, some teachers are still holding onto an outdated classroom structure that does not serve their students well.

In many ways, students are the same as they were twenty five years ago. They are still social creatures. They are still motivated by a challenge. They are still self-directed. They are still trying to feature their strengths while hiding their weaknesses. And they are still bored stiff when the teacher drones on endlessly. What is different about students is their expectation of what will occur in the classroom. When kids experience a self-directed, open-learning classroom, they begin to expect that type of classroom at each level of their schooling. Students and parents begin not only to expect but to demand a classroom structure that benefits the kids on multiple levels. Not only do they expect to learn content but also to learn the skills and processes they will need in order to succeed at the next level of school and the next stages of life. This is where "20% Time" is playing such a vital role for our kids.

During the Idea Showcase (one of our "20% Time" project events that I will discuss later in this book) last year, some teachers from our building came down to browse the kids' projects. After being amazed at the quality of project ideas, one teacher said to me, "Wow, we really have to up our game in eighth grade! If you're doing this kind of thing in seventh grade, they're going to expect something similar when they get to eighth grade." She was exactly right. We have to keep pushing in order to personalize the learning and make school the place kids **want** to be.

We teachers have to realize that we are now competing with various learning platforms. In my opinion, YouTube has done more to transform learning than anything else. If a student wants to learn how to do something, they simply search for a YouTube video. Heck, I do the same thing. There are millions of hours of free learning at every kid's fingertips. Other providers, like Khan Academy and Lumosity, have capitalized on the desire for people to learn independently. Now there are dozens, hundreds, maybe even thousands of places to acquire knowledge and kids will take advantage of all them. The classroom may have become the place where kids learn the *least*, and this is where we are failing them.

In order for us to meet the kids' classroom expectations, we must change. We must break out of our decades-old model and incorporate a more democratic approach to learning. We have to use online resources, technology, play, independence, personalization, the kids' expertise and energy, and anything else we can think of to get kids excited and learning. When kids see value in coming to our classes, they will want to be there every day.

Kids today are not that different than kids twenty five years ago. They still want a safe place to learn. They still want to be challenged and recognized for their learning. They still want a hand in creating their learning and they still want to be able to use available technology to learn. However, the kids' expectations of school have indeed changed. Now they expect to find a classroom that better suits their needs and learning. It is not the students who have changed. Rather, it is the structure of the classroom that has changed. Because we are in the middle of an educational revolution, albeit a slow one, we are better able to serve our students on a variety of levels and make school the place where kids want to be. This is what "20% Time" has done for us on Harmony Team, and what it could do for you.

Preparing for Yesterday

We have all been in those meetings where we thought, "What in the name of all that is holy does this have to do with my kiddos learning?" I was recently in a curriculum meeting like that. In this meeting, we were "tweaking our social studies assessments". It seems like every time we meet, we "tweak the assessments". The assessments are always content-oriented paper tests that come at the end of a unit of study.

At one point in the meeting, our coordinator, who is very progressive and as frustrated at the focus on the old way as I am, asked us, "What if we made the test into a Google Form and put it online?" I perked up a little. Last year, I had put one of the assessments on a Google Form and given the assessment to the kids that way.

"Well, we'd have to turn off the wifi after the kids had the form," one of my colleagues said.

"Why would we turn off the wifi?" I asked.

"So they don't Google the answers," another colleague said.

"I put one of these tests on a Form last year and let them Google answers. If they could find the answer on Google, it shouldn't be on the test," I replied. From the looks on their faces you would have thought I'd just ordered the killing of a hundred puppies. No one, except our coordinator, was in any mood to hear that! After all, why would we want to change assessments from simply plugging regurgitated facts into something that strengthens the students' abilities to critically and independently think? Ludicrous!

Therein lies the problem. We as educators keep doing the same things over and over again. Once in awhile, we change the window dressing a bit but it is still essentially the same things that we were doing ten or twenty years ago. Do these things improve students' learning? Nope. Why do we keep doing them then? Because *it's the way we've always done it*. We slog through, tweaking the content a bit or the form the content takes, but we don't fundamentally change our practices. Instead of reading a textbook, we put that textbook online so kids can read it there and we pat ourselves on the back and proclaim ourselves mavericks and techies. This is innovative because the kids are reading the same content on a screen instead of in a book? Really? That's all we've got?

Traditional schooling is destined to fail our kids. Some modes of education from twenty years ago are only preparing kids for the world and careers that existed twenty years ago. They don't prepare kids for the world of today, much less the world of tomorrow. Our kids will be graduating into a world that no longer values book knowledge but rather problem-solving, creativity, design and intellectual agility. Our schools need a revolution. We need to throw out all that we know and begin building from the ground up. I like to ask other teachers, "If you were to completely redesign a learning environment for kids, with no restrictions, how much would it resemble our current school system?" Not one teacher ever told me that it would be close to what we have today. We know in our hearts that we are going down the wrong road but we feel powerless to stop, reverse course, and begin the process of change so that kids can experience real learning.

We have to approach our teaching with much more urgency. We have to know that these kids leave us in a precious few months and we may not have adequately prepared them for the world in which they will live. We may have prepared them for the next grade level of school but there is little resemblance between the next grade level and the skills they will need for their lives after school. Yet we hold on to the past, teaching with the same methods that would be recognized as good schooling in classrooms 100 years ago. In fact, **we are preparing the kids for yesterday.**

In my district, there is great autonomy and taking risks is valued. Many teachers in my district are experimenting with methods and programs that are actually enabling great learning. Why aren't we all? Many have reached the "comfort zone" which in my opinion is the most dangerous place to be. The teacher becomes comfortable doing the same thing year after year and yet wonders time and again why the kids are not responding like they used to. The kids resemble silent, bored automatons, slogging through their daily chores in order to get to that final bell that allows them to leave school and begin learning what is really important to them.

The "comfort zone" is the worst place to be. It is paralyzing for the teachers and it is especially detrimental for the students. Once a teacher reaches the "comfort zone", and has no intention of leaving it, it is time for them to retire. The "comfort zone" is not conducive to learning for either the teachers or the students. The only way we grow is to learn new things. If we never reach out to try new things, then we never learn anything new. To be sure, if we have done the same project for the last fifteen years, something is drastically wrong. The teacher is not learning and growing and, as a result, the students are not learning and growing. It is through the teachers' new learning that the students will grow and learn. It is true that the "comfort zone" is easy for the teacher but it is absolutely the worst thing for the kiddos.

I NEVER want my kids to be eagerly awaiting the end of the school day in order to escape, go home, and learn more about their interests and things about which they are truly passionate. I want to empower them with the secondary and tertiary skills necessary to figure out *their* best way to learn, work out a plan for this learning, and begin the process of finding the right resources to create and discover. I want the kids to collaborate in order to experience learning more than they would have if they were tasked with learning in isolation. Work is becoming more collaborative everyday and the kids must have the skills to thrive in that type of environment. I never want my kids to experience the "comfort zone"; simply doing the same thing over and over again because it is easy and routine. There is no growth there. There is no development there. There is no learning there. It is only by stretching that we achieve anything of value.

In my 28 years of teaching, there have been dozens of "solutions" to the problem of kids' lack of interest in school. We have tried program after program, but what they all had in common was that they gave kids no say in their own learning. We adults decide the best learning for the students. Because the kids had no stake in their own education, every one of those programs was destined for failure. Why should kids care about learning what the adults chose to put upon them? They may have no interest in it even though many of the teachers are very interested in it. The kiddos think, "Who cares? It has nothing to do with me." They are right; it has nothing to do with them. It is no wonder that they are so disinterested.

Only when we personalize learning (and by personalize, I mean give kids a stake in the planning and execution of their own learning), will we make significant progress toward giving kids a real education. As adults, do we take classes in which we are not interested? Of course not. For those who went to college, did someone else choose their majors? Of course not. When adults go home from work, do they enter into hobbies, book clubs, or other learning events that they hate? Of course not. Adults choose their own learning. *Why do we expect kids to be okay with not being able to have some choice in their own learning?* If an adult were told to go through seven hours of classes that held no interest for them, they would quit after a day. Yet we expect, no, we *demand* that kids do it. This expectation has killed off the excitement of learning for so many students.

The bottom line is that kids want to learn. They may not want to learn what we have to teach them, but they want to learn. When a kid acts up in class, it can be a sign that they are not getting what they need in class. Many times, when a kid does not do an assignment it means that the assignment had no relevance to them. When kids seem distracted or mentally absent, it may mean that school is not a place that holds their attention. There has to be a better way to engage kids in learning that really matters to them. There has to be a way for us to harness the natural curiosity and creativity of kids and use that curiosity to teach skills and content that kids will really use in the future.

There is a better way - personalized learning through "20% Time". Personalized learning allows the kids a hand in constructing their own learning. They will see learning as both challenging and fun. They will see the usefulness and value of the things they are doing. The kiddos will feel a sense of accomplishment when they finish a learning task because they will have learned something important *to them*. When kids feel a sense of pride because of something they accomplished, they will want more in order to experience that feeling again. In time, we will have reawakened their love of learning and in turn we will have created and nurtured lifelong learners. These learners will know how to approach a problem, analyze it, research it, prepare a first solution, tweak that solution, refine the solution, communicate the solution in a way that makes sense, and finally publish that solution. This is the kind of education that the kids will need in order to thrive in their world. If we personalize their learning, we can make sure that the kids are well-prepared to live in that world. If we personalize their experiences, then we can truly cultivate their genius.

The Lone Ranger

Every teacher at some point in their career experiences being alone in their thoughts and views of education and school. Believe me, Melissa and I have gone through our times of being outcasts in our own school. There are times when every teacher thinks, "There is so much more I could do for my kids if I could just throw off these limitations and focus on what's important to them." We all go through it. We feel like we are caught in a system that moves too slowly, one that has too much bureaucracy, and one that does not give us the time or freedom to introduce really impactful programs. We feel alone.

It is easy to get down on ourselves and feel like a failure for knowing what would make a difference with our kids but feeling powerless to do anything about it. Administrators often do not want to allow change because they are afraid it will "rock the boat". Why change now? The way things have always been done are the way things have always been done. They are tried and true and our kids are performing well enough to "get by". But shouldn't we as teachers want more for our kids than just "getting by". We should want them to reach for more, fearlessly attempt great things, and learn from those attempts.

What many teachers do in situations where they feel no support among their colleagues or from administration is close their doors and do what they feel is best for their kids. They experiment with different things and assess how the kids respond to those new ideas. These teachers do this experimentation on their own to see what works. This is how Melissa and I brought "20% Time" to our students and further reinforced our status in our building as the rebels and outcasts. This is how we earned ourselves "Lone Ranger" status.

It is difficult to maintain a mindset of positivity and energy when you feel alone. However, the energy that the kids infuse into a classroom, especially when they know you are trying something different for their benefit, will give you all the support you need. "Hey kids, we are going to try something different. No one else in the school is trying this. We'll be the first! I think it is going to help us learn better and will be a lot more fun than what we were supposed to do." Phrased like this, you will hook them every time. They will go the extra mile to ensure the success of the project. They love being pioneers and innovators. They love feeling that they have a stake in their learning environment. While the rest of the faculty may not be especially supportive, if you engage the kids and let them know they have a voice, the kiddos will definitely give you the support you need.

Knowing you have the kids on board is amazing, but it doesn't negate the reality that we as teachers are accountable. Even Melissa and I, our building's Lone Rangers, know that. When we began implementing our first iteration of "20% Time" we knew there could be raised eyebrows. When administrators ducked in with questions about what we were doing, we often embedded our experimentation under the umbrella of "Action Research". This terminology bought us time to develop our "20% Time" program. By the time they checked in again, we were able to point to successes and show some data about the learning. Most of the time, the data will open things up for teachers to try more new things in class. Soon, word will get out about what you are doing, that you have some support (or at least permission) from the administration, and other teachers will warm up to the idea and come around to see what you are doing. A few will buy in and begin to collaborate. Soon, the circle expands and you've put together a whole team of like-minded teachers. The Lone Ranger has become collaborator, rather than outcast.

Does this scenario really work? Yes, it can. When Melissa and I started, we told our principal in passing what we wanted to do. He didn't really understand it or where we wanted to take it (and to be fair, we weren't really sure where it was going either), so he didn't say "no". We took that as approval and ran with it. Other teachers in our grade level didn't get what we were doing. We had always been a little more "loose" with our classrooms because we personalized our teaching and did more project-based learning. The prevailing view of our team was that we were the "party team" and we never did any work. We constantly heard this from kids on other teams, and our kids heard it too. "Oh yeah, my teacher said you guys don't really do anything. You just play all day. We do real work," they echoed.

We tried to chalk up this judgment to a lack of understanding among our colleagues, but the digs still hurt and they hurt our kids. No one wants to be on a team that is viewed in such a negative light. We told the kids over and over that they were doing work that mattered to them instead of just school work. We told them that the world does not work like schools. We told them that in the real world, you don't get information to memorize for a test. In the real world, you're given a problem to solve and you normally have to work with others to solve that problem. We knew we were the Lone Rangers in our building but we were convinced that "20% Time" was a way of learning that was worth any negative assumptions that others had. Soon our determination and dedication began to pay off.

Word started getting out about the cool projects that our kids were doing. We have a few events, what we call "high stakes days", where kids showcase their progress and exhibit their learning. I'll talk about these later in the book, but they are basically checkpoints that we opened up to the school, the families of the students, and the rest of our district. We were trying to build community support both inside the school and outside the school. When kids from other teams saw some of the projects, they began to say, "Why can't we do stuff like this?" The tide was ever so slightly beginning to turn.

When our first group of "20% Time" veterans went on to eighth grade, they excelled at problem-solving and technology use. After all, a big chunk of their seventh grade year was all about solving problems, getting past barriers to their learning, and using lots of devices, apps, programs, and other technology. The most difficult thing for this group of kids was returning to a more traditional classroom setting. They were used to solving complicated problems, creating their own learning, and presenting those solutions to others. They had overcome their anxiety about failing and were fearless. Many became bored in situations where they could no longer engage in that kind of learning. Memorizing facts to regurgitate on a test was no longer what school meant to them. "20% Time" had succeeded.

Since implementing a "20% Time" culture into our classrooms for the past several years, attitudes and perceptions of the "party team" have definitely changed. These days Melissa and I are frequently sought after to help a teacher implement a "20% Time" program that is tailored to his or her situation. We give professional development sessions to groups of teachers who want to learn about or develop a program for their own class or school. We even speak at conferences about "20% Time". Indeed, the tide has turned. A few years ago, we were the Lone Rangers. We don't feel so alone anymore.

The Second Person

A few years ago, I saw a YouTube video where a man was dancing all alone at a concert. Commenting on the video was a sociologist who suggested that this man would not be able to get the rest of the people around him dancing, but a second person would. Sure enough, after a short time of dancing alone, another man entered the picture and began dancing near the first man. Within a few minutes, others joined in until the area was full of people dancing.

The sociological significance of this scenario is that while many of the people probably thought that the first man was a "yahoo", a "weirdo", or some crazy lone ranger, and even though they may have wanted to dance, they wouldn't for fear of being a "yahoo", too. But once the second man entered the picture, the first man was validated. Then others began streaming in, not because of the first man's epic dance moves, but because the second person showed them that is was now socially acceptable to come over and dance.

This scenario demonstrates the power of what I'll call the "second person". Every school has a teacher who will try anything, no matter how ridiculous it sounds to others, in order to get through to the kids. That teacher is not restricted by convention and relies on feedback from the students to tell them if what they are doing is working. Despite the risk of failing, they are willing to go out on a limb to try something new in the hopes that it will benefit their students in some way. When another teacher joins in, that first teacher is validated. Soon others will begin hovering around, trying to see what is going on. It won't be long until the dance floor is packed.

For a long time at my school, I was the "yahoo" out there dancing to the beat of my own drum…alone. I was that teacher who would try various things to hook the kids, much to the chagrin of some of my colleagues. Now to be fair, many of my colleagues said, "Go for it!" However, they would not join in and or try some of the things I thought would work. They kept doing the same things that they'd been doing in the past, which is completely fine… if it works. Not me. I get bored doing the same things over and over. Whether it was a long-term project, a writing process or even gaming and creating, the kids in my class always played a role in what they were going to learn. I listen to the kids and often direct learning based on their verbal and nonverbal feedback. This has lead to a unique physical environment as well. My room decor was always reflected what I thought helped kids to feel comfortable and ready to learn. For a long time, while other teachers stressed "neat desks in neat rows" I had couches and easy chairs. Now, I have tables painted with Dry Erase paint and office chairs that rock, roll and swivel, giving the kids not only physical freedom to move around and work together, but intellectual freedom to grab a marker and work through a thought or problem while sharing it on the table with their neighbors. We have to keep in mind that kids need to move so we need furniture that accommodates that movement. This all ties back to my belief that how we teach the kids and enable them to teach themselves should be based on what they need, now what we want them to have. Even with things like classroom furniture, I was a lone ranger. However, a "second person" sure would have been nice - someone to talk to and collaborate.

When Melissa came to Hixson, I saw a kindred spirit. She was not one for doing things conventionally just because that's the way things had always been done. Granted, she was a new teacher who had but few points of reference to the way things had always been done; but there were other characteristics that let me know I could lure her to the dark side. She was full of ideas and she was dauntless. She didn't just accept things at face value. She wanted to know "Why?" and if there was a better way to do things so that kids would be more engaged and learn better. She became my "second person" and I became hers. Now, no matter how crazy my ideas were, she was on board to try. It was when she began starting sentences with, "Okay, I know this may sound crazy, but what if we…?" that I knew things were about to get interesting. When Melissa walked into my room on that fateful August morning before school and said, "Hey, I was watching some TED Talks last night and came across 20% Time. It's something I want to do. We can do it as a team or at least I want to do it?" I knew we were destined to do some very good things with the learning environment on our team. I jumped at the chance to be her "second person" and help launch what has now become one of the highlights of our team, school, and district, and one of the things, in all of my years of teaching, of which I am most proud.

With each other as our "second person" we began developing our "20% Time" program to fit within the restrictions of our school day. For starters, we knew we could each give up one class during the week. Also, we knew we had to make it work for fifty kids. We also knew we were limited on space so whatever we did needed to be able to work in our classrooms. Aside from these conditions, the sky was the limit! From that point forward, anytime we came across something that could be a problem, we began troubleshooting immediately. Our response to any idea was, "Why not?" We didn't let fear stop us if something had never been tried before or if there was a chance that others might frown upon it. If we thought an idea would open things up for the kids to learn, explore and create, then we gave it a shot. More of those shots hit the mark than missed it, but "failing forward" is part of the journey. The important part is learning from each attempt and pushing to make the "20% Time" experience rewarding to the kids.

In the last year, we have heard from a lot of teachers who say, "I wish I could do something like that, but I just have _____ _____ that keeps me from trying it." Those teachers fill in that blank with various reasons why "20% Time" WON'T work for them. If you ask me, I think one of the biggest reasons why it "WON'T" work for them is that it's hard to do anything new and do it alone. Nobody wants to be the Lone Ranger. To be sure, Melissa and I have a great situation. Our administration has been either supportive or laissez-faire, our kids' parents were open to the adventure, and Melissa and I have had each other for "second person" support and motivation. However, no matter what restrictions or roadblocks were put up for us, we found a way to implement "20% Time". It was just that important to us.

Climate Change

We frequently tell kids, "Just wait until you are in the real world!" The current attitude surrounding education is that it is an artificially created entity that is separate from this "real world" to which we so often refer; the real world is made up of everything else. Well, I have news for us all; the kids have been in the real world since birth. We like to separate school from this fabled place but to the kids, it's one and the same. It is educators, administrators, parents and a host of others who have set up this atmosphere for learning, trying to segregate it from all other aspects of the kiddos' lives. This artificial "climate control" is unrealistic and potentially detrimental to the students. To kids, school is as much a part of their real world climate as anything else. It is where they learn, explore, socialize, and figure out how to define themselves in society. We as adults need to start recognizing this and using it to help the kids reach their full potential. We need to embrace an educational climate change that integrates all aspects of life.

The educational paradigm that needs to keep schools separate from the real world was constructed ages ago to make efficient, obedient, task-oriented robots because that was the skill-set that kids needed once they entered the workforce. In a society that did not have easy access to information, the teacher's role was an important one--the sage on the stage. For most kids, they could not get answers from their parents and books were not as available as they are today. Kids could learn a great deal of factual information from the teacher. After all, who knew better than the teacher? Even as someone who grew up in the 1970s, I remember having limited access to books. I had some access to books because I was a semi-regular visitor to the public library. For those who didn't visit the library, schools (and teachers) were where books and information were available.

Nowadays, the educational climate is experiencing a dramatic shift. Kids have access to more information than any teacher could possibly provide, and this information is not just school-specific. Kids can research anything that interests them. They have a wealth of instantaneous knowledge at their fingertips. Got a question about alligators in Florida? Google it! Want to know how to change the SD card on your phone? Watch a YouTube video tutorial and learn it in a few minutes. Kids now have the ability to be very specific about their learning, often preferring what is immediately interesting to them to the limits put upon them by the curriculum or test-mandated knowledge that stifles their natural curiosity, creativity, and thirst for knowledge.

Initiating an educational climate change that embraces new methods and resources can be difficult. The system is trying to take advantage of the advent of information technology, but the practices have not yet become mainstream and breakthroughs are happening faster than they can be adopted and adapted. Indeed, we as educators are finding our way and making plenty mistakes as we go. We are so used to working within the existing paradigm that it is extremely difficult to break out of it. We are no longer the experts on everything. We are no longer the only resource our kids have for learning. We MUST construct a new paradigm based on ALL of the tools that kids can now access in order to enrich their learning and allow them to be their own sources of knowledge. We need an educational climate change!

One thing that we can do to change this paradigm is admit that we teachers do not have all of the answers. We can't possibly have all of the answers! We need to own that and use it to our advantage. Kids are curious and they want answers now. We should not slow down their learning simply because we don't know. By telling kids that "We'll get to that later" or "We're not going to learn that this year" it is only forcing them to stifle their own desire to learn. We MUST honor kids' natural curiosity and allow our students to pursue learning that matters TO THEM. We need to keep them engaged by empowering them to become the expert. We have all had to sit through things in which we were not interested and caught ourselves watching the clock, hoping that we could will time to move faster. In my sophomore Spanish class, I would follow the second hand around each minute, daydreaming as it spun. Ask me today how much Spanish I know and I can scrounge up "un poquito" but not much else. Does this mean I was a bad student, or could it be that what I was expected to learn held no pertinence to my 15 year old brain? Either way, I can tell you Spanish class was one of the longest hours of the day.

Time always seems to move more quickly when we are engaged in things that are interesting to us. It is amazing how slow the clock moves, both for the students and the teacher alike, when the learning seems artificial and contrived. It is only when we hit on something that gets everyone in the room jazzed up that time moves like a race car. It is a very special class that gets the kids so excited that they moan and groan when the bell rings because they want more. The other day, we received a 3D Doodle Pen (handheld pen-like 3D printer) and one of the students wanted to take it out for a test drive. He was near my desk in the back of the room trying it and after about two minutes, I looked up from helping a student to see five children around him watching him use the pen and creating a list so that they could all take turns using the pen. At the end of the class period, who do you think was most regretful that the bell rang to end class? Of course, those kids who were participating in authentic, relevant, spontaneous, collaborative learning.

We should strive to make all of our classes like the time with the 3D pen. They have to be periods of discovery, both self-discovery and discovery of the world around them. To be sure, we have to help kids achieve learning goals, but those goals should be created collaboratively with participation from both teacher and student. Once we create these goals, the kids will achieve more because the learning is THEIRS. They had a hand in planning it and they took their natural curiosity into account.

By collaborating with the students to create their personal learning goals, we are blurring the line between "school" and "the real world". This is what makes "20% Time" so important to Melissa and me. The kids get absolute freedom to choose something about which they are passionate. The hours spent in class become time that kids are truly motivated to discover and learn. Indeed, the paradigm shifts because kids see value in coming to class. School has now transformed into a place where they can try out new things in a safe learning environment. They don't have to worry about whether their first attempt at learning is successful. They are free to "fail forward" and pick themselves up and try again after a big flop. This environment is the one we need to create in our schools because once we give the kids the reins to drive their own learning, their potential is endless. If we are always telling the kids about the "real world", why not let them help shape the world in which they live? We have more resources to empower them now than ever before. We just need to do it.

Classrooms must become laboratories of learning. We must open things up so that students can pursue their learning using the tools that fit them best; tools that allow them to demonstrate their mastery of the learning that truly matters to them. If things don't work for a child, we must endeavour to find what does work. We CANNOT keep putting irrelevant (to the students) assignments in front of the kids and expect that they will be eager, interested and driven. We CANNOT punish them for not being the students WE want them to be. We need to embrace this educational climate change so that WE can become the teachers THEY need us to be.

This change will not be easy. There will be times when we wonder, "What am I doing?" There will be times when we think we are failing. But how can we teach the kids that it's okay to "fail forward" if we demonstrate a fear of exploration in front of them? There will be times when we will want to pull out our hair (I guess I am lucky that genetics took care of my hair years ago). I used to come to class thinking I had created a really cool project idea, something that took me hours of thought and preparation, and inevitably the kids would amend, tinker or revamp it every time. Now I have embraced this collaborative effort between myself and my students. I give them the starter idea and they have the creative freedom to tailor that idea to their own learning. As with anything, there will always be a few kids who fritter away the time. They find websites that make funny noises. They hack game sites. They change the settings on their computers so that everything reads in Japanese and spins when a certain button is pushed. Sometimes, I take a step back and really look at a kid who appears disinterested and I realize that he could be the creator of the next "South Park" or "Minecraft". Another student who is constantly hacking his computer could go on to work for NASA. I know what I am teaching is not interesting to everyone and I don't take it personally. I sit in awe of their abilities and realize that I just need to support their learning and make sure that we work their skills and interests into our classroom program. This is why Melissa and I know in our hearts that "20% Time" is a great tool that will allow us to drive our own climate change.

Every teacher will find the environment that works best for them and their kids. What works for us may not work perfectly for someone else. I would never be so deluded as to think that my classroom runs smoothly all the time. We still struggle with our time and space and what we are learning. But the important thing is that we are trying. I say "yes" more often than not to kids who ask if they can reach their goals in a way different than the methods prescribed by the district. I work to get the tools our kids need in order to experiment, dabble, work, play and learn. In our environment, everything is on the table because I want kids to leave their year with me knowing that they succeeded at learning what really mattered to them and better yet, that they were good at it. I want the kids to know that their ideas have value and that each of them does have genius within them. Mostly, I want them to know that learning is fun and something they WANT to do for the rest of their lives. If I can do THAT, then in my mind, I have successfully initiated a positive climate change.

The Mess of Learning

Occasionally, I walk down the hallway and peek into other classrooms. Many times I see very quiet students, arranged in nice straight rows, focused on the board or performing tasks the teacher gave them. There is a place for everything and everything is in its place. Some students are intent on finishing the tasks while others put their heads down, stare out the window, or just look blankly around the room. My initial impulse, even after all of these years, is jealousy. I admit it. I'm a teensy bit jealous that some teachers have mastered the art of keeping the kids silent during class. It may be a throwback to how schools used to be and sometimes I think it is how others still want school to be. After all, quiet kids show that work is being done. Or so they say. But then the brief moment of envy passes and I realize that this classroom model doesn't reflect who I am as a teacher or the things that I want to nurture in my students. When it comes to my teaching style and my students' learning styles, it is fair to say that we are "the mess" of the school.

I've always had one of the "louder" classrooms in my hall, but I've always felt that there has to be conversation around learning and sometimes those conversations get pretty loud. Is this good? Well, for my classroom, yes. As for "nice, straight, little rows", well, let's just say that learning in my room happens when kids dig into the learning. They use the MakerSpace, they immerse themselves in coding with the Raspberry Pi, they build with Legos and they lose themselves in research.

The disparity between the silent and neat classrooms I have observed and the noisy, messy classroom that I have shows that we are different teachers and use our talents in different ways to get the most out of kids. Now don't get me wrong, I'm not saying that for some teachers, the quiet and orderly environment is a bad thing. We all teach according to our strengths, and we should. Kids need different experiences as they go through their days. As for me, I learn through active conversations that include bouncing ideas off of others and thinking out loud. Simply put, I learn loudly. I know that there is a time and place for quiet reflection, focus, pondering, imagining, dreaming and wondering. We do a lot of that in class, but when it comes to quiet work or independent reflection, isn't that something that could be done…well, independently? When we are in class, we are a group of 20-25 individuals, each with a different point of view and unique skill set or expertise. Shouldn't we use this time together to increase our collective genius? Since we are all together in class at the same time, I figure we should also do much of the collaborative work there. When kids have productive conversations, they get excited. They get noisy, they move around, and things can get messy. It's not necessarily misbehavior or intentional disruption. In my experience, it is usually just over-exuberance from the excitement at the exchange of ideas or the creating that is taking place. This occurs on a daily basis in my classroom, and during "20% Time" more than ever. This is the mess of learning. This is the mess that I love.

I don't kid myself, though. In teaching middle school, I work with 12-13 year olds. I know that not all of the noise I hear and mess I see is because the kids are engaged in a meaningful and deep exchange and exploration of ideas. Sometimes they are just being crazy. But this is something you see no matter what kind of lesson you as a teacher plan. There will always be that small handful of students who are goofing off, wasting time, or not paying attention, whether it is during "20% Time", silent reading time, or working on a worksheet. This is the nature of the beast. There are times when I have a class that has to be reined in more than I like because the group cannot stay focused enough to learn. If the noise becomes a detriment to learning, then we find other ways to collaborate. For Harmony Team, this can include dividing into smaller groups, moving kiddos around, or using devices and engaging the kiddos with apps. In my opinion, the worst thing to do is to throw out the collaborative piece because of too much noise. Problem-solving through collaboration is an increasingly necessary skill to have and kids have to learn how to effectively do it using their talents and skills. It is now the single most essential workplace skill and the more we can cultivate that skill in class, the better off the kids will be later in life.

We adults prize quiet because that is the type of school environment in which we were brought up. Many of us think that if it was good enough for us, it's good enough for the kids. What we need to realize is that we don't look back upon those silent times as our most memorable school experiences. Instead, we look back at the projects we did, the field trips we took, and the collaboration we had as the most memorable (and dare I say, fun) experiences from school. It is the experiential and interactive learning that stretched our thinking and fired up our imagination. In this respect I believe students today are the same as they were 10, 20, 50 years ago. But again, change can be scary and many stick to the "tried and true" educational models within the classroom walls.

While change can be scary, one thing that is common through the ages is that human beings are social creatures. Anthropologists believe that our social collaboration is what has led to our evolution as one of the dominant forces on the planet. From sharing simplistic teachings about stone tool production to developing group hunting strategies to organizing revolutionary endeavors in engineering to conceiving the advent of microchip, technology that vaulted us into the modern era, all of our successes can be linked back to our ability to share ideas and improve upon "the way things have always been done". We need social interaction to grow and learn. In fact, more and more technology is being introduced every day that fosters social interaction and connecting. We must take this quintessential human trait into account when we plan our school experiences and learning activities. Kids must know that we value the learning aspect as well as the social aspect of school.

Sometimes this socialization can involve strange noises and messes. Learning is not clean. The classroom full of kids who silently read and neatly write answers to questions is not a classroom that is fostering innovative learning for most kids. Does it help with memorizing facts long enough to regurgitate them on a test and then forget them? Possibly. But is that the learning we need moving forward? Learning can get messy, and that's ok! Each student must come to know how they learn best. For some, that is reading. For others, it's listening or watching. For many, it is by experiencing. A classroom that really fosters learning will have all of these things going on at once. Some kids will be in a corner reading, others will be debating, some might be drawing, some will be listening to audio or watching video, and some will be focusing on their classmates and learning from them. All of the kids will be striving for a mastery of something but doing it in a way that benefits them the most. Believe me, this type of classroom is not a silent one, and it is not the easiest one for a teacher to observe. A classroom where all of the students are potentially working on different projects or different facets of a general idea can be hectic, chaotic, noisy, messy, disorganized, and a little crazy. This is the mess of learning.

When we allow kids to learn how they learn best, we also make managing that type of classroom more difficult, and this can sometimes seem like we are making an already difficult job nearly impossible. The teacher must become an individual guide to each student in the class. By definition, this type of classroom transfers the work from the teacher to the student. The students, using their talents and skills, are now responsible for learning and mastering. This learning is messy and it's noisy, but it's great for kids. They take ownership of the material, they take ownership of the way they'll learn, and they take ownership of how they will demonstrate their learning. The students are in charge of their learning; the teacher becomes a guide and resource.

Redesigning our classrooms into active learning environments means letting go of the reins. It means saying "yes" much more than "no". It means nurturing ideas and allowing kids to explore. It means allowing kids to dive headfirst into their learning. It means allowing them to make a splash. When Melissa and I embraced "20% Time" and, as a team, fostered this type of learning, we saw that the kids were not only exploring their individual projects, but they were also mastering active learning. Kids also learn secondary skills like organization, building connections with those outside of school, and engineering ways to demonstrate what they've learned. These secondary skills will benefit kids as much, if not more, than the learning we might have originally intended for them. Since we have introduced "20% Time" the kids have been a little noisier and a little messier. For us this just further affirms that we have made the right decision for our kids. They are engaged, excited, and joyous about learning again, and sometimes in middle school that can result in volume and motion. If that means a little mess, then I am okay with that.

The Lead Learner

When we change our classes to a Project Based Learning (PBL) format and introduce "20% Time" to the kids, we also change our role in the classroom. Traditionally, teachers have been "in charge" of the kids' learning. Teachers made the decisions that would best suit the kids and move them merrily on their way towards achieving learning goals that were set by everyone but the students. Teachers designed and orchestrated the work that kids would undertake and the kids would complete that work and turn it in for a grade. But our role as teachers is changing. The sooner we embrace the change, the better we will be. With kids demanding a more open environment where they get to make their own learning decisions, teachers need to evolve. Certainly, there are some teachers who never will; there are some teachers who will cling desperately to the old days where their place in the classroom was secure.

We must transition to become the "lead learner". We have to demonstrate to the kids daily how we learn, how we fail and how we succeed. We must introduce things to kids KNOWING that we are not the expert. It is okay to be the person in the room who knows the least about something. We want to raise the kids to be lifelong learners, yet we are afraid to let them see us learning. No one is born knowing everything and this includes teachers as much as it does students. We must allow the kids to bring into the classroom things that matter to them. This type of environment leads to a lot of uncertainty and let's face it, uncertainty can make even the best of us a little anxious. That's okay. When we understand that we are not supposed to know everything and that it's ok to be out of our comfort zone, a huge burden is lifted from our shoulders. We, like the kids, become active learners in the collaborative classroom.

The most powerful words I utter in class, usually on a daily basis, are "I don't know. Let's find out!" When I tell kids that there is something I don't know, but want to learn it, then the atmosphere in the classroom changes. It is no longer about the teacher knowing everything and the student measuring themselves against that standard of knowledge. Now it is about everyone trying to learn together. It is about kids being motivated to learn in order to help their fellow students and their teacher. This motivation is intrinsic because the desire to help others is intrinsic. Kids look up to their teachers and feel a sense of pride when they are able to help someone they look up to and respect. The kids like the feeling of validation. We capitalize on this motivation to get kids learning.

When our kids are working on their "20% Time" projects, Melissa and I learn a great deal. Last year, our student, Kaiden, built a solar-power golf cart. He did all of the work: soliciting a donation from a solar company, creating a "Go Fund Me" to buy a golf cart, and building the cart itself. Another student, Musa, decided that he wanted to create a self-sustaining ecosystem in a pond located on his family's land. Musa researched everything and created his ecosystem, and it worked. I don't know anything about how solar power works. I also don't know a lot about ponds and water ecosystems. As the kids learn, so do I. It is much more powerful for the kids when I ask them genuine questions about their projects. I am not asking because I have a quiz in my hands and I am checking their knowledge against content they are "supposed" to learn. No, I am asking them questions because their projects are cool and I am really interested in what they are doing. Kids can tell the difference between "teacher questions" and real, authentic questions about their projects.

When kids begin to see themselves as experts, the shift in their enthusiasm and energy is palpable and contagious. They find value and pride in their new designation. Suddenly, Kaiden is the solar-power engine expert in school. He takes that status seriously and it not only helps him in his 20% Time project, it also helps him see himself as a serious learner, leader, and innovator. Then we just sit back and watch how this confidence carries over into his other classes and his life outside the school walls. Kaiden will probably perform better in all of his classes because he now sees himself differently. Kaiden also finds more value in himself and the love of learning that can vault him past what traditional school models can offer. We have taken a big step in creating a lifelong learner who has a growth mindset.

I have had to give up my idea of what a teacher is "supposed to be" and have found myself learning and failing right along my kids. I have had to check my ego at the door and realize that what should be highlighted is what the kids are doing, not what I am doing or saying. I have had to use what they bring into the classroom as both the content and the medium through which we learn. I have had to allow for the natural collaboration that takes place in a "20% Time" program specifically and a PBL classroom generally. I have had to relearn that we have 25 curious, imaginative, creative experts in the room and I should rely on that expertise. We have truly become a team of learners, sometimes muddling our way through uncharted territory and always celebrating our victories. We are in this together, none more so than me, the lead learner in my class.

Personalized Learning

Our team at school is named Harmony. We chose that name because it represents what we want for our kids, our team and ourselves. Harmony is the state of balance and agreement. We named our "20% Time" program Harmonized Learning because we want kids' learning to be in harmony with the kind of learner they are. Our mission is to tailor the learning to every individual in every class every day, to really personalize the learning.

For years we have heard about differentiation. Then came individualization. Neither of those methods is as effective as personalization. We define differentiation as tailoring instruction to accommodate students that are at certain levels. We differentiate our instruction to the high, middle and low achievers. We try to reach all kids in class because the hope is that all of the kids will fall into one of the categories. Individualization is different because it tailors instruction on an individual basis when differentiation isn't working for a student. Those not "getting it" in a differentiated classroom must then be approached individually.

The problem with differentiation and individualization is that the flow of learning and work is from the teacher to the student, whereby the student remains a passive receptacle of instruction. Students listen to or watch the teacher "teach" about the topic of the day. The classroom dynamic has not changed, it has only been narrowed down to focus more individually on each student. These attempts at individual instruction demonstrate good teaching. But a more effective way to teach is personalization.

Personalization of learning has all of the benefits of individualization. The difference between the two is that with personalization, the student has an active role in designing the learning and the learning outcomes. The students take the lead in their education. They make decisions about their instruction. They choose how they will organize themselves, what resources they will use, what their timeline will be, and how they will demonstrate their learning.

When I first transformed my classroom into a personalized learning environment, kids were resistant. "This is not how school works!" they decried. "You're just doing this because you're lazy!" they denounced. "You're supposed to stand up there and tell us what we need to know and then test us on it!" they cried. Class became very uncomfortable for them because they had been trained in the old system to be passive learners. They knew the game of school. Teacher gives material, teacher helps kids understand material, teacher prepares test to ensure kids understand material, teacher administers and grades test, and everyone moves on to the next unit. The only common denominator in this process is the teacher. This paradigm is not one that encourages learning among students. Melissa and I, along with thousands of progressive teachers around the world, want to change all of that. We want our role as teachers to change and we want the role of students to change as well. We want kids making some of the decisions that every learner should be making.

On Harmony Team we talk about the learning goals at the beginning of a unit. What are we supposed to get out of this unit? We discuss what we should master, what is essential to know, and what is good to know just because. I make available to students an array of resources (video, audio, print, online, etc.) that the kids can use in order to achieve their learning goals. Kids immerse themselves in the learning, making their own decisions about how they will learn. We have a lot of kids who prefer video as their learning preference. Others love to read stories. Some will listen to podcasts as they do other things. The idea is that each student, with the guidance of the teacher, makes the decisions about how they will learn best. Many times, that decision is made because of a learning disability. A few years ago, Justin, a quiet student, had problems in the classroom because of his dyslexia. He used a "voice/text" app that not only allowed him to speak his writing assignments but also allowed him to "hear" the text resources. By giving kids opportunities and choices in their learning, we can accommodate any learning challenge a student may have.

Students can find the balance between the type of learner they are and how they approach learning. This balance is instinctive and it is this balance for which we strive, knowing that when kids figure out their abilities and strengths, we have done a better job of preparing them for life beyond our classrooms. We are trying to teach skills to the kids that will be with them for the rest of their lives. Personalizing students' learning is a great way to teach the classroom content while also teaching the secondary skills necessary to become lifelong learners.

Decisions, Decisions!

One of the reasons we LOVE "20% Time" is because the kids must make so many decisions about their learning. On Kick-Off Day, they begin making dozens of decisions right away. During the hour or so that we initially give them to brainstorm ideas, many kids will fall in and out of love with no less than five different ideas. The interesting part occurs when the decision to further research a specific idea falls squarely on their shoulders. Melissa and I make it a point not to guide or coax any of the students in a particular direction or towards a specific idea. The decision MUST be theirs. When students change their ideas, it is the result of a decision that they made. One boy, Jimmy, had a difficult time coming up with a project but knew he wanted it to relate to sports. Eventually he created a website, blog and podcast tracking the offseason transactions of NFL teams. Ethan and Yensen, friends since elementary school, decided to work together creating a new kind of candy. A month or so into their project, they went their separate ways because Yensen realized that she wanted to research sleep disorders instead. Another student, Owen, didn't know what he wanted to do until one day he joked about creating a new kind of food, the Panaffle. That "joke" became a reality for Owen. He had one of the most well-received, and tastiest, projects. Some kids change their ideas because they are not able to secure the resources they would need for a particular project, or because they are not invested in the idea anymore. We allow the kids to change their ideas because it takes time for some kids to figure out what they really want to learn.

As adults, we make decisions that affect our lives everyday, but for kids, this thought is exciting and revolutionary when all they've ever known is a system where adults call the shots. Students usually don't make decisions about their learning. In a normal school setting, the teacher gives a pre-planned paper assignment to the child, posts a due date and lets the kids work on the assignment, answering questions along the way. On the due date, the students (most of them) turn in the assignment for a grade. The student receives the grade within a few days and the process begins anew. After nine months of this arrangement, the kids are dismissed for summer vacation.

This model that most schools still follow does not allow for students to make many, if any, decisions about their own learning. I have told many of my students that if I had to follow a student's schedule for more than a day, I'd go nuts. That system is not designed for how I learn best. What decisions does a student make in the course of the school day? Whether or not to do and turn in the assignment? Whether to use a pen or pencil? Whether to daydream before working or after? Kids are unprepared to make any decisions about their learning because we don't LET them make any decisions about their learning. We treat them as children who are incapable of deciding anything. This is a disservice to the kids. By not giving them practice making decisions and accepting outcomes in a relatively safe environment, we are setting them up for failure when they eventually have to make decisions down the road. When we provide a safe environment for the kids and allow them some decision-making power, they will begin to take a more active role in their learning. They will fail sometimes but they will pick themselves up and try again. They will gain confidence in themselves and learn to persevere.

When we kick off "20% Time", the kids' lack of decision-making ability is painfully obvious. When we release them to begin thinking and creating, many fall flat on their faces. That's awesome! We pick them up and give them some encouragement and guidance and let them go again. Some fall time and again. Cool! For Melissa and me, the more times they fall down, the more practice they have getting back up. The biggest problem they have is not being able to decide what to do. Can't we just assign them something, they ask? We explain that the whole point of the project is that it is THEIR learning, not ours. We are through assigning things for them to do. They must come up with this one on their own.

Why is this decision-making process so hard for our kids? Well, one problem they face is that they put artificial boundaries on their learning. They think, "What would the teacher expect?" and try to think within those parameters. We play a cruel trick on them by explaining to them that we have no parameters; they can do pretty much whatever they want. It does not have to be tied to the curriculum in any way. Talk about culture shock! Now the burden is back on them; they really have to think of an idea about which THEY are excited. The kids who have mastered the "memorize, regurgitate, repeat" system are stymied. Buh-bye comfort zones! Suddenly, the work is THEIRS, not the teacher's. This really blows their minds! The training wheels are off!

The kids literally have to make hundreds of decisions during their "20% Time" projects. First, they have to decide on a project. For some, this can take days, for others, weeks. There are a few for whom it has taken the entire duration of the project. Next comes the penultimate question (at least in their minds)...Will they work alone or with someone else? Do BFFs make good partners? That's up to them to decide and accept the outcome. If they do work with someone else, a whole new plethora of decisions must be made. How will they begin their project? Who will be their mentor? What do they hope to accomplish? How much time will they spend on their project at home? What materials will they use? Where will they get those materials? How will they fundraise for the money to buy those materials? Who will be in charge of what? Each day during "20% Time", kids are making decisions. They have to. No one else will be doing it for them. There is no Mr. Eckert or Mrs. Hellwig who will come in and show them how to do the assignment. We simply answer their quandaries with more and more questions. This is when the real growing and learning begins. For the record, we have begun to discourage partners because we were finding that many kids were more passionate about a partner than an idea.

During the "20% Time" experience, we are not the most helpful teachers. That sounds like an odd statement but it is true. Kids come to us all of the time hoping that we will bail them out of a tough situation. They cannot decide between two roads their project could take. Could we just tell them which road to take? Of course we could, but will we? No, we won't. If we did, then whatever the kiddo was working on stops being theirs and starts being ours. The kids struggle with these decisions and we love seeing it. There is no way we are stepping in and delivering them from a tough spot. This project is theirs and so everything tied to it must be theirs as well, including any decisions that have to be made. When kids start making these decisions and seeing some of them work and some, well, not so much, then taking charge of their own learning feels more normal to them and they begin to own it. As with everything else in life, it is only with practice that they become adept and mature decision-makers. They can never and will never be confident decision-makers if we make all of the decisions for them or step in and save them from having to make hard choices. Two years ago, Andrew and Macy were partners but Macy didn't think Andrew was invested in the project. She wanted to break from Andrew and do the project on her own. Melissa said, "Fine, but you will have that talk with Andrew. I will be there with you, but you have to do this yourself. I'm not doing it for you." It was difficult but Macy talked to Andrew and they went their separate ways.

The best thing we can do for the kids is help them focus on a project of their choice and get out of their way as much as possible. We will help students refocus by asking questions but as soon as we start making suggestions about the way we would do the project, it becomes less their project and more our project. Not intervening is a tough skill to learn, especially when a teacher really cares about their students and wants them to succeed, but for the students' sake, we must learn to step back and watch the struggle. It is only through this struggle that they grow as learners, and one of the first obstacles they need to face and overcome on the way to becoming lifelong learners is deciding that they are able to succeed.

Innovation Knows No Grade Level

Since Melissa and I have implemented "20% Time", we have gotten a lot of feedback and questions from elementary school teachers. They are interested and excited about starting "20% Time" programs in their classes but often have questions about how that would work. They understand that at the seventh grade level, kids can be reasonably self-directed and motivated. They are not sure how elementary school children would react to an environment with less constraints and more freedom, especially since most children need more guidance and set routines. Our answer to them is that it is never too early to teach kids that they can be "geniuses", especially with young children who are naturally creative and curious, and who haven't yet learned to be afraid.

    I propose that starting in the early elementary grades is important in order to properly acquaint kids in the kind of learning and discovery they will be doing for the rest of their lives. When students get to middle school after having been indoctrinated with a "traditional" classroom model, Melissa and I must help them unlearn the idea that "quiet" and "neat" are of paramount importance and that their purpose in school is to memorize arbitrary content to be ready for Friday's test. This makes things like PBL, Genius Hour, and "20% Time" so much more of a challenge. The kids have to relearn what it's like to be inquisitive and creative without the teacher telling them what they "want" or "need" to learn. If the kiddos came to us from a school where their elementary teachers had already begun introducing them to a classroom model which gives them ownership in their education, then they would be better poised to aim for the stars.

There are some elementary school teachers in our district who have come to us and we have helped them implement a version of "20% Time" in their classrooms. They have tweaked the program to fit their specific needs and situations, taking into consideration the time and space they have to devote to "20% Time" in order to garner the most benefits for their students. Yet it is the format, the ideology, and the philosophy of "20% Time" that is the most essential aspect for the kids to learn. The students need to live "20% Time" in order to fully understand it. Parents need to see their kids both thriving as well as struggling in this environment to fully grasp what it means for their children's education. One of the biggest roles Melissa and I play in this "20% Time" culture is building up support in our school and community for the kids so that they have every opportunity to succeed.

When we are approached by a teacher asking for guidance in implementing a "20% Time" program into their classroom, the first thing out of our mouths (aside from "AWESOME!") is always "start small". We advise teachers to phase in a program that is smaller in nature and build on that program gradually. Melissa's and my situation was unique in that we had two teachers and fifty kids. Together we built our framework first and then filled it in with the various learning activities and events. We created as we went, sensing and adapting what our next step should be based on how the kids were responding. Teachers who are doing "20% Time" for the first time may need to do the same. FedEx Days or Genius Hour projects may be good ways to introduce the "20% Time" mindset to kids. It was these elementary school teachers, who wanted to empower their kids and adopt a "20% Time" learning environment, who inspired me to write this book. In the second half of the book, I provide step-by-step instructions about how Melissa and I started our own "Harmonized Learning" environment. I also share with you all of the forms, documents, matrices, and supplemental material you may need to develop your own "20% Time" program.

FedEx Day is a one-day problem-based project that is a manageable introduction to "20% Time". Students are given a relevant problem (how to curb food waste in the cafeteria or implementing a recycling program in school) and have 24 hours to come up with a solution and present that solution to the class. Kids collaborate, research, and when they are done, explain to their teachers and peers why their solution is the best.

This past year, our FedEx Day centered around a new laptop roll-out event for our one-to-one initiative. The previous year, our roll-out was a disaster. Not all kids got their computers, the people-management system we used was awful, parents were standing in long lines, the paperwork was never turned in and it was a general mess. Melissa and I charged our students with developing a process to run a smooth roll-out that involved both students and parents, using the time and space we had at our school. Kids spent the following 24 hours browsing the building, researching, debating, collaborating and creating presentations of their solutions. The problem was immediate and relevant to them and they knew they were working on a tight deadline.

In addition to FedEx Day, we have also suggested Genius Hour to teachers as a great way to try out a "20% Time" classroom environment without making such a long-term commitment. Genius Hour is a project that usually span four to six weeks. The process is similar to "20% Time" in that kids have to come up with their idea and then research, create, innovate, and present their learning. When one Genius Hour project is complete, the process repeats itself. Indeed, a teacher can run 6-8 Genius Hour projects in any given year. Genius Hour may be an easier way to develop the mindset of kids as lifelong learners without committing to a full year program, especially for very early grade teachers.

Whether you decide to test the waters by exploring FedEx Days or Genius Hour with your kids or choose to dive right into a "20% Time" educational atmosphere, the key is to find the format that best serves the students at each grade level. All kids are innovative regardless of their age. All kids want to succeed. When we, as teachers, stand back and give them the freedom to create and innovate, they will blow our minds. We have an obligation to nurture that creativity, not kill it. We can't say, "Oh, well, '20% Time' will be great for the kids when they get older." The kind of learning that "20% Time" represents is beneficial for kids at any grade level and at any age. Sometimes, it is the youngest children asking "why" that stimulates the best ideas. Sometimes it is the limitations that we put on children that can be the most damaging to their development. If we could realize that kids of any age are amazing thinkers and problem solvers and if we as adults could understand that innovation truly knows no grade level, then our students would thrive in the environments that we create for them.

Failing Forward

From the moment they begin school, children are taught that one of the greatest measures of academic success is knowing facts and answering questions correctly. Going one step further, if they really want to be a star, they should be able to do these things quickly. From multiplication table races to timed exams, the current educational model has always valued and rewarded students who could memorize content and exhibit this 'knowledge' quickly, usually in the form of some quantifiable assessment. We as educators have always valued knowledge and the fast, accurate display of that knowledge. It impresses many of us. Traditionally, there has been no room for "perceived" failure in the classroom, and it is precisely this definition and expectation of success that is crippling our students.

Our children, because of these standards, learn early on that creativity and passion should be packed away in favor of memorization and recitation for fear of being viewed by their teachers and peers as a failure. I mean, the worst thing you can be in life is a failure... right? Wrong! From Thomas Edison to Ben Franklin to the Wright Brothers, failure has played a huge role in creation and innovation. It is rare that one succeeds at something the first time they do it. In a "20% Time" environment, failure is valued. We know that we learn more from our failures than we do from our successes. Failure often breeds success. It is all a process. Try something the first time. Fail. Try again. Fail. Try again. Succeed. The keys to success are the effort, analysis, thinking, imagining and innovating that go into the solutions to the problems that turn a failure into a success. In the long run, is any failure that we learn from really failure?

No child wants to hear that they failed at something. I don't know any adult who enjoys it either. The difference between adults and kids, though, is that kids often personalize the failure and see it as a value judgment on them as human beings. They feel that they are not good enough or smart enough. Now, the truth is that for a few, failure in the traditional sense motivates them to try harder. They will work harder, study more and answer quicker. They try to prove that they are good and earn approval from their peers, teachers, and parents. But more often than not, failure can be a crushing blow to kids. In their minds, failure defines them because, since it came from an adult, they accept that assessment as truth. The kids may now approach every problem as someone who is a "failure" without trying to tap into their natural brilliance to solve it. That is why "20% Time" is such a game-changer.

When we talk to the kiddos about failure, we explain the difference between "good failure" and "bad failure". Good failure is when we test out an idea and it doesn't work out because of something unforeseen. Bad failure is when we don't put any effort into our work. Good failure is a great learning experience and we value it for what it teaches us. Bad failure is when we try something, encounter a problem and give up. With good failure, we tweak what we do and we eventually come up with a solution to the problem. During "20% Time", and on Harmony Team in general, bad failure is the only failure that we don't accept. It is not the actual "failure" that is bad, it is the student's lack of effort or reaction to that failure that we need to address. After all, since these projects are imagined and designed by the kids, they are motivated to work on them and put in as much effort as necessary. That is what makes "20% Time" so successful. Since the kids are at the helm of their own learning, it is rare that we see bad failure in our students.

Our kids learn to embrace the concept of "failing forward". Failing forward is when a person TRIES TO solve a problem, VENTURES TO create something new or STRIVES TO innovate and hits a roadblock. The attempt may have ended with a failure, but if that child takes that unsuccessful endeavor, learns from it, and approaches their goals anew with a fresh perspective, then that is failing forward. Quitting is an example of bad failure. The real spirit of failing forward is believing in yourself, examining what went wrong, proclaiming that you will not give up, and going forward fearlessly with new information to solve the problem. This isn't always easy to do and it does involve a lot of hard work and determination, but then again, doesn't everything that is worth doing?

What is one of the easiest ways that we can inspire our kids to courageously fail forward? We can let them in on the big secret, that everyone is a failure at some point in their lives. We all fail, some of us many times a day. We like to use successful innovators as examples to show that anything is possible, but we rarely talk about the dozens of attempts that those innovators made before coming up with their groundbreaking idea. If kids never see the people they admire failing forward, how are they ever supposed to feel comfortable with the idea of failing themselves? This needs to start with us in the classroom so kids can appreciate that failure is just a first attempt in learning.

In our writing classes, we use the Workshop Model, which is a lot like "20% Time". We tell kids all of the time not to worry about their first draft. The first draft, I tell them, is just the clay that they will mold into something special. The kids come to understand that we expect them to make mistakes on their first draft. We use their own pieces of writing to teach them the skills of writing. Through the process of revision, the kids learn how to make their writing better and eventually they achieve a final draft. This process is not magic. It is work. No one expects a professional writer, let alone a student, to be able to produce a final draft the first time they write something. If we accept this expectation for writing, why don't we accept it for all other learning as well? We should.

During our "20% Time" program, Melissa and I constantly talk about failure. The kids get used to the idea and it is not a scary word to them anymore. They know that if they fall down, they pick themselves up and try again. There is no shame. There is no judgment. There is only learning. If that learning takes three attempts, awesome. If that learning takes twenty attempts, wonderful. The important thing is for the kids to feel comfortable in their environment so that they can make attempts at learning, knowing that if those attempts do not turn out right, they can always regroup, find the support they need, and fail forward again. When we as educators are able to move our kids to this place, it will be a huge success for all.

Gaming is Learning

One of the most exciting things to me about teaching right now is being able to watch and experience each new and exciting development in educational technology. When our school was deciding what kind of computers to purchase for the building-wide 1:1 laptop initiative, they included Melissa and myself in the decision-making. We had already written grants and acquired a full class set of Chromebooks for our Harmony Team kids a year earlier. We had decided to go with a relatively new laptop, Samsung's first generation Chromebook, and our tech gurus were interested to see how they worked. We loved them, but aside from the actual computer, we loved the fact that now each one of our students had the full reach of the internet at their fingers. With "20% Time" this proved beneficial because it opened up the students to so much more information than we, or our school library, could have provided. But kids will undoubtedly be kids and along with all of the perks of having a computer in every student's hands for exploration, inspiration, and research, now there were 25 gateways with which our kids could goof around, be distracted, and (insert GASP here) GAME!

Now, I don't want to blaspheme or say anything too incendiary, but I want to get the point across that gaming can also be learning. Now, the kiddos may not be learning exactly what we want them to learn, but they are learning. We know that there is something about figuring out a puzzle that draws people in. We all love it, kids and adults alike. We are all up for the challenge. If you think about it, games provide the best kind of learning. Kids will enthusiastically try to win the game or solve the puzzle.

They will work tirelessly because it is a challenge. They feel like there is an opportunity to accomplish a "win". If they don't make it, what do they do? They immediately try again and again and again. In fact, they try until they actually win the game. How much would we teachers give to have a classroom full of kids who showed those qualities when it came to the learning we wanted them to experience? A lot, I'll bet. In fact, it is the holy grail of education and I have tried to inspire this enthusiasm in my students for the past three decades.

When Melissa and I changed the class structure to a more Project Based Learning class and introduced the "20% Time" program, I knew that my role as teacher had to change. One of the ways I decided to adapt as a teacher was by realizing that I wanted to tap into the tenacity that kids show while gaming. In my mind, it wasn't Mr. Eckert vs. Gaming, but rather Mr. Eckert harnessing the powers of Gaming and using them for good! For example, in our social studies class I found several games that revolved around Classical Greece and Rome. One game, Fling the Teacher, is a trivia game that allow kids to design their teacher character and catapult that teacher if they answer some Roman trivia questions correctly. I know that kids were motivated to learn the Roman content so that they would be able to fling their teacher character, which incidentally often looked a lot like me, as far as possible. Another game, Dress the Roman Soldier, gave kids an opportunity to dress a gladiator so that he would not die in a fight. The game made the students learn about how gladiators dressed for fighting and allowed them to demonstrate that learning. If they didn't learn it well enough, their gladiator died and they had to try again. Another game was an archaeology game called "Dig It Up" where students learned all about Roman artifacts while their cartoon figure dug through ruins, finding all kinds of things along the way.

During this class period, the kids were focused and intent on winning the games. Sometimes, a couple of kids collaborated on different strategies that would ultimately succeed and some would troubleshoot until they figured it out on their own. NOT ONE kid felt like they were a failure if they didn't win the game. They simply tried again. That tenacity and acceptance of "failure as a first effort" are characteristics that I want my kiddos to exemplify on a daily basis. When their mindset changes from "I got it wrong so I am stupid and will never be good at it" to "I got it wrong this time but I know I can get it" then I will feel like we have succeeded in helping nurture a growth mindset. The kids will be well on their way to becoming lifelong learners. For me, it starts with trying to incorporate some tenants of gaming into the classroom because when the kids game, they learn fearlessly.

Gaming taps into the kids' own intrinsic motivation, the same motivation that we are trying to access in our classes and our "20% Time" program. We want our students to be motivated by THEIR work, not by rewards or promises from us. We want kids to OWN the work. When they do, their self-image changes from "student playing the game of school" to "individual learning something that is personally fulfilling". Gaming is a great demonstration of the way we want kids to view learning. We want them to try, fail, and then keep trying until they succeed. We want them to be excited, tenacious, determined, and fearless. Gaming is a great model of this mindset towards learning and it is up to us as teachers to access this model and apply it in our everyday classes as another tool in our arsenal to help students achieve greatness.

It Only Takes a Spark to Ignite a Flame

The following is a blog post that Melissa wrote in April, 2014. It sums up our thinking about the start of this program and how 20% Time should lead to a different way of doing things in schools.

I know we usually talk about our students and how their 20% Time Projects are going for them, the struggles we have encountered or successes we have celebrated. However, today I want to talk about the motivation, both personal and professional motivation associated with the undertaking of this project and the unforeseen positives that have come from the 20% Project.

This year has been personally and professionally motivating and encouraging. I started off this year feeling discouraged, wanting to change my classroom parameters, but I didn't know how or what to do. I stumbled upon this idea of 20% Time, Genius Hour, FedEx Day in a Google Community and one thing led to another. I spent hours watching Ted Talks (particularly Daniel Pink's talk here), reading blogs (check this one out) and chatting in Google Communities. I was inspired by the idea of students taking control of their own learning and choosing their own learning paths. In this model, they get to pursue a passion or interest that they have always had but maybe never had the means or opportunity to pursue. 20% Time was going to help get kids to love learning again!!! Motivate them! Ignite that inner flame of motivation that could follow them through the rest of their lives, creating a life-long learner.

We have been so amazed by what some of our kids are doing with their projects: raising money for cancer patients, building a go-kart, or starting an environmentally-friendly fishing lure business. More importantly, I have satisfied my own inner motivation personally and professionally. Don and I have always taught this way but always behind closed doors, only collaborating with each other for fear of someone wanting to stop us in the type of teaching that we truly believed in. We knew that some people said that we "never did or taught anything" just because our students enjoyed being on our team or in our classrooms. For me personally, that was always hard to hear. Those comments never threw Don and me from our path and we kept trudging along.

Education is changing and it is time for teachers to start jumping on the bandwagon. Our students, more than ever, are growing up in the Information Age, where every answer is at their fingertips. When we can answer a question with the click of the mouse, why are we making that content the basis of our curriculum? I understand there was a need when access to that type of information was limited but that is no longer. Curriculum needs to be changing with the needs of our students. As teachers, we need to sit down and truly look at what is most important and what is good to know. This is a hard step for any great teacher because we learned, when we were students in school, the traditional way to teach. When we went to college we learned the traditional way to teach, and so when we entered our career most of us clung to the traditional way to teach. It is hard to let go of what you know and what you are comfortable with. It is scary to try something new in a classroom where you might fail or it might not work, especially if you aren't in a school culture where you are encouraged to try new things. There was a time and place for traditional teaching (and there still is at times!) but as the world is changing, schools must change to do justice for our students. We need to prepare our students for 20 years in the future, for jobs that haven't even yet been created.

I feel motivated now more than ever that the way I am currently teaching (I have changed what I was doing even from just a year ago!) is the correct path for my students. Our students need skills like problem-solving, perseverance, critical thinking, social media skills, computer (or device) research skills, etc. Is content awesome to know? Absolutely! But does our whole curriculum have to based upon the content anymore? I would have to say "No". For example, this past week a student asked me in science, "What is the reason our hands or feet 'fall asleep'?" I told them I didn't know the answer but asked if he had his device. He did and I told him to find the answer for us. What an awesome feeling this was and it was liberating as a teacher!

The role of the teacher has changed to "facilitator of learning" from "teacher-led learning". We need create a culture of passion, love, and interest for our subjects while also allowing students a place to feel safe to "fail" and try again. What this project has brought into me professionally could have never been foreseen. It was the spark that ignited the flame for me in my teaching. I encourage every teacher to be the spark for your school. Get your peers to jump on your bandwagon because what you are doing for your students will have long-term effects on their learning. If you believe what you are doing for kids, keep doing it. It is hard to be the outlier but eventually you will be in the majority.

The flame, for us, has been transformational. We took all of our pent-up motivation and all of our ideas for a more ideal learning environment and created the "20% Time" program that I outline in Part 2 of this book. Every year we tweak the program but the second half of this book will provide a great starting point. Part 2 is the practical part of the program, the nuts and bolts, the roadmap and the materials you will need in order to create and implement your own "20% Time" program. I explain every part of the program in detail and include the forms and sheets we use in order to administer this program. Please feel free to modify all of the forms for your own learning environment. I hope that the second half of this book gives you a head start in your planning. I must warn you that once you begin this journey, your teaching career will never be the same.

Part 2
Our "20% Time" Program Template

Planning the Learning

We know that "20% Time" is a way for students to use a portion of their class time to pursue personal learning goals that are inspired by their passions and intrinsic motivation. The question that remains is "How do we do it?" The following chapters form a template for educators to use, revise, tweak, or overhaul to fit their own situations. Considerations of time, space and colleague involvement are essential when planning an effective "20% Time" program. Over the past several years, our program has evolved into what we feel is a terrific fit for our unique situation. We know that our program is ever-changing and every time we encounter an obstacle or a pothole, we must adapt and modify our program even further. The standard that we keep in mind is to always do what is best for our students, and that can change from one year to the next. In a way, the mental flexibility that we hope to cultivate in our students is being honed in ourselves each time we have to re-shape or modify our program. I hope our vision of "20% Time" can become a jumping-off point for you to mold into a best fit for you. I encourage teachers to take from this book what they want, amend what needs to be adjusted, and reject what will not work for them. After all, education is all about sharing and I am excited to share our ""20% Time" program with you.

Our "20% Time" program runs nearly the entire school year. We start in October with Kick-Off Day, a time when we gather the students together for a talk about what "20% Time" is and what we would like them to do. From there, we begin investigating ideas. After a few weeks, we get ready for Pitch Day, when kids must "pitch" their ideas to a committee, a la "Shark Tank". Kids continue to work on their projects after Pitch Day and in February, we hold the Idea Showcase, a gallery walk of projects that is open to the school community. Kids continue their work during spring semester and we conduct a few Checkpoint Activities to make sure the kids are making progress. At the end of the year, in May, we host an event called Student TED Talks. Each student will give a five-minute TED Talk, in the auditorium, on stage, about the learning that occurred during their project. While this is a rough outline of the program, each of these events will be discussed in detail in this section of the book.

We have included the documents that we use with the kids for each step of the process.. We show our own working calendar of events, the letters that we send to parents to help keep them involved and up-to-date, planning notes, and other relevant "behind the scenes" documents that might be helpful for teachers to use as a starting point. We also share the templates that we use for our "high stakes days", like Pitch Day, Idea Showcase, and our penultimate TedTalks. One of the keys to the success of "20% Time" is how well the teacher prepares for the first month, including Kick-Off Day. The success of the first month is crucial for creating a positive snowball effect and allows the kids to really explore their own learning. Not only will teachers create a program, they will also create a learning environment that will grab their students from the beginning and light a fire in them to take control of their own education. It is this fire that will continue to burn and motivate them to cultivate their genius in your very own "20% Time" program.

Sample Planning Sheet and Calendar

As I have mentioned before, planning and preparation on the part of the teacher are essential to the success of the program. This was one of our first calendars of "20% Time" work and events. It was a collaborative document that we tweaked as the year progressed. We changed the dates and events as needed. It was a very fluid document and serves as the basis for our program every year. This is an up-close look at various segments of a "20% Time" program.

"20% Time" Planning Sheet

Calendar of Events: These dates often coincide with regular "20% Time" days in Don's and Melissa's classes. Don runs "20% Time" during social studies classes every Monday and Melissa runs 20% Time during science classes every Thursday.

- 10/1/13 - "20% Time" Kick-Off Day
- 10/1/13 - Parent Letter sent out
- 10/5/13 - Socratic Symposium on "failure"
- 10/15/13 - The Bad Idea Wall in Science Classes
- 10/20/13 - Create Harmony Team 20% Blog (to link to kids' blogs)
- 10/24/13 - Introduce Blogger to kids
- 11/4/13 - Students do idea-generation activities
- 11/11/13 - Students begin blogging weekly
- 11/16/13 - Students begin preparing for Pitch Day
- 12/8/13 - Pitch practice
- 12/15/13 - Students pitch ideas to team 1 min video; some time to answer questions from panel Create the checklist of what panel will look for for the graded part; give this to students ahead of time to prep; get with Kathy about putting extra people (Jim, Lana, extra sub in the building that day, Bodi, Alice?) with kids while pitches are taking place. Switch lunches? Get Jason H, Merlene, John S, (Jill, Don, Melissa)
- 1/25/14 - Begin preparing for Idea Showcase - Requirement: Poster; create the criteria to give to groups ahead of time

- 2/16/14 - Idea Showcase of 20% Projects - Have mentor sign-up sheets available
- 2/28/14 - Mentors secured by each group
- 3/12/14 - Checkpoint Activity 1
- 4/1/14 - Critique TED Talks for effectiveness in English Classes
- 4/25/14 - Checkpoint Activity 2
- 5/5/14- Sign up for TED Talk time Create a calendar for sign up
- 5/10/14 - Organize TED Talk schedule
- 5/16/14 - Project Presentations (TED Talks) in Auditorium Talk. Videotaped and posted on blog.

Announcement Day Background

"**20**% Time" may change from year to year to best suit the needs of each group of students. This need for flexibility doesn't just apply to the program in general, but also to each of its composite parts. For example, the process for Kick-Off Day may change slightly from year to year, but the overall goals are the same. Perhaps the most crucial part of Kick-Off Day is getting the students comfortable with the idea of inquiry based lessons. We encourage them to try and figure out what "20% Time" is on their own at first.

After 10-15 minutes of kids researching the topic, we take questions and then share the following "rules" with the kids.

- Kids will spend 20% of our class time, or every Monday in Social Studies and every Thursday in Science, working on their 20% Time projects.
- Kids must work individually unless there are two similar projects and the kids want to combine into one project. The passion must come from the work, not the partner. We discourage working in pairs or groups because, in our experience, most do not work out.
- The kids are responsible for the entire project.
- We stress that the kids should choose a project that is new and not something they would normally do in school. They are free to research other 20% Time learning projects to get ideas.
- Kids must show their learning. Not everyone creates something but many do. This project is more about the learning than anything.

Even if there is not enough time for kids to produce a project, they will still have learned a great deal in the process.
- Kids must "pitch" their proposal to a committee of educators. The pitch must include a purpose, audience, timeline and resources they will need to complete the project.
- Students will also present their project idea at the Idea Showcase, a gallery walk of student "20% Time" ideas. The Idea Showcase is open to the school community.
- Kids should have a mentor. Many times, adults who come through to view the project ideas can mentor a student because of their expertise.
- Students must keep a blog where they will reflect weekly about their learning.
- If at any time kids are feeling overwhelmed, they must schedule a time to meet with the teachers to figure out a way to organize things to be more manageable.
- The last project is a student TED Talk.
- Failure is an option. Learning from our mistakes teaches us a great deal.

We tell kids that we are not grading on the product. We are grading on the learning that came from the project. We cannot penalize kids because they did not have enough time to accomplish a product. We talk about various checkpoints along the way where we will be grading them and leave it at that. Too much information during this kick-off would be overwhelming.

The next day in class, we give the kids time to ponder, discuss, imagine, research and dabble with different project ideas. We refrain from offering advice or ideas because we want this project to be THEIR idea.

The Letter to Parents

There are many factors that will affect how smoothly you can incorporate "20% Time" into your classroom. Of all the things that influence the kids' receptiveness to this innovative approach to school, parental buy-in and support are perhaps the most crucial. If we can get the parents excited about this great opportunity, then their enthusiasm can help steer the children to approach "20% Time" with a positive attitude. Melissa and I always make it a point to prepare the parents for a different kind of school experience. We give them as much information as is needed to help them understand the adventure we are taking their children on and what we hope the kids will get from it. We explain our plan, we point them to additional resources, and we make ourselves available at any time if they (or their children) should have any questions. We understand that when the kids are faced with something that takes them outside of their comfort zone, it isn't just difficult for them; it is difficult for their parents as well. They want to help their children when they are stumped, and in order for them to do this effectively, it is our job as teachers to help them prepare for the questions they may encounter when their kiddos come home after Kick-Off Day. This is the letter that we send home to parents.

> Dear Team Harmony Parents,
> We wanted to write to let you know a little bit about one of the unusual projects we'll be taking on this year. The "20% Time" project is a major inquiry-based learning project that spans the rest of the year and encourages students to pursue a creative interest

they would otherwise not experience in our academic program at Hixson Middle School.

Before we get into the details of the project, we want to explain why we're asking students to participate in this activity. For over twenty years, a trend in education has been gaining momentum that suggests the role of the teacher should shift away from an industrial model where the teacher stands in the front of the classroom to dispense content through lectures and the students sit to consume that information. Rather than being the "sage on the stage" as some pedagogical experts maintain, teachers increasingly ought to play the role of the "guide on the side". In this role, the students play a much more active role in how the content and knowledge is acquired. In this model, teachers provide resources, ask questions, and suggest projects for students to explore. While we may play the "sage on the stage" role in some of our class, the "20% Time" project is one place where we will always be the "guide on the side". Put simply, this is a student-centered project rather than a teacher-centered project.

Another crucial element in designing this project is intrinsic motivation. We recommend *Drive: The Surprising Truth About What Motivates Us* by Daniel Pink. We cannot recommend this book enough. You can get a taste of it by watching his TED Talk called *The Puzzle of Motivation*. In fact, one of Google's business tenants included "20% Time" and during this time, employees created some of the best Google products to come to market (Gmail, AdSense, etc.). The book explains why the same principles apply to education.

How does the "20% Time" project work?

It all starts with brainstorming. In October, students will begin brainstorming ideas for a project proposal. Students may work alone or they may work in pairs if they have similar ideas and can combine into one project. While brainstorming, we will encourage students to shoot for a product, though a product is not absolutely necessary. Kids will be creating graphic novels, computer-powered gadgets, social media campaigns, athletic events, films, books, videos and games. The point here is that after the idea simmers, we move from the idea phase of this project to the production or creation phase. Even if kids never get to the production stage, they will have learned a great deal by shooting for that stage of the project.

Proposal

Once the student has an idea of what project they want to pursue, they begin writing the proposal. The team will "pitch" the project to the Pitch Committee based on their written proposal. In the proposal, kids should address the following questions: What is your project? Who will work with you on this project? Who is the audience/client for this project? Why is this project meaningful to you? What do you expect to learn from this project? What product will you have to show at the end of the year? What sort of expenses will be involved in your project and how will you cover them? What equipment will you need and where will you get it? What is your timeline for completing (or launching) your project?

The Blog

Each week, every student is required to write a blog post where they discuss their progress. They write about what happened over the past week, what they learned, what challenges they faced, and what they anticipate in the future. Students will show one of the teachers their blog post in draft form before posting.

Mentors

We would like to see each student find an adult mentor who can help guide and inspire them. We hope parents will play a role in finding an appropriate mentor for this project. The mentor will offer advice, provide informal leadership, and follow the progress of the blog.

The Final Presentation
At the end of the year, each team will give a five-minute presentation to students, teachers and community members during which they will show their learning. This will be carefully written and rehearsed to produce the best presentation they have ever given. These TED-style talks will be delivered and recorded in the auditorium.

Assessment
Many students and parents understandably ask about how we are going to grade the "20% Time" project. We try to de-emphasize the grade because extrinsic motivators like grades tend to discourage the innovation and creativity we are looking for in this project. We want them to be inspired by the project itself, not by the grade they're going to get.

With that being said, we are going to assess students on various elements of the project. A significant portion of their grade will be dependent on the following elements with rubrics: the Pitch, the blog, the Idea Showcase, the Checkpoint Activities, the product, productivity, and the Student TED Talks.

What if my project is a failure?
The world's best entrepreneurs embrace failure. The only true failure is lack of effort. We want students to strive to show off a successful product at the end of the year, but even if there is no product, the Student TED Talk can still be a successful talk about learning. We remind kids that they are not striving for failure but they should not be afraid of failure either.

We are excited about all of the different things we're going to be doing this year on Harmony Team, and we can't wait to be amazed, surprised and inspired by the innovative projects this year's students will produce in the "20% Time" projects. If you have any questions about anything, don't hesitate to email us at melissahellwig34@gmail.com or doneckert314@gmail.com. You can also message us on Twitter @melissahellwig4 or @dayankee.

We are documenting this whole "20% Time" learning process on our team blog harmonizedlearning.blogspot.com. Please check in. There will be a link on the blog to our weekly podcast as well. We are very excited to begin this learning adventure. Please come along for the ride!

Sincerely,
Melissa and Don

The Kick-Off

At the beginning of each year, our school has an evening where parents and students can come in, walk the building, and meet the teachers they will have that year. This is called Open House, and it is always such a great night. We get to meet the parents of all of our new students, introduce ourselves and learn as much as possible about our new kiddos. Since we only have fifty kids between the two of us, we usually get all of the parents in one room and do an interactive presentation about the year ahead. We don't talk much about the curriculum. Parents don't come to Open House to hear about the curriculum. They come to Open House to see who will be taking care of their children for up to eight hours a day. We talk to parents about how we will get to know the kids, the relationships we will build with both them and their children, the great work the kids will do, and the culture that we will build on team. More often than not, by the time we are finished, we have about a dozen parents asking if they can come back to seventh grade. Open House is indeed a very validating and fun evening for us.

One of the projects that we mention during Open House is "20% Time". We talk a little about the theory behind the program, the format of the program and what our expectations are. We mention a few of the projects from the last couple of years and then ask the parents not to talk much about it to their children. Inevitably, the very next day, at least ten kids come in asking about "20% Time". "When can we start?" "Are we doing '20% Time'?" We ask them if they know what "20% Time" is and usually they say "no". They just know it's really cool because some of their parents couldn't keep it to themselves. For a couple of months, we tease them a bit with off-hand comments about "20% Time", said with a mischievous grin as if we know something amazing that they don't. These comments are usually met with kids asking, if not begging, for more information. Leading up to our Kick-Off Day, the excitement and expectation is almost palpable.

Finally, in October, we plan a big kick-off for "20% Time". We block our team schedule so that we have a 100-minute class together and gather all of the kids in one room. We start by playing a few TED Talks. We play the Daniel Pink TED Talk called "The Puzzle of Motivation", the Ken Robinson TED Talk called "Are Schools Killing Creativity?" and the Logan LaPlante TED Talk called "Hackschooling Makes Me Happy". Now, the Logan LaPlante video is especially intriguing to our kids because Logan was thirteen years old at the time of this talk. He talks about how traditional school failed him and how much he is learning and how happy he is by creating his own school experiences. The kids start to get excited. We do nothing to dampen that enthusiasm. We want them as jacked up about learning as possible.

After showing the three TED Talks, we talk to the kids about what "20% Time" is, how we fit it into our school week, and the kinds of things they can do with the time. We have a presentation that we show the kids. In this presentation, the kids are introduced to some of the key dates they will need to prepare for, some requirements of the program, and some of the projects and blogs of previous students. "Wait! Wait! We can make a go-kart???" one student shouts. "Sure. Why not? You want to?" I reply. Well, of course, every kid wants to make a go-kart like the one a student group made the year before, but very few have the drive to really make it happen. They do, however, have the drive to make THEIR passion happen. The trick is to cut through all of the initial false starts and get to what really motivates them. That process is long but we don't tell the kiddos that just yet.

It's funny; not once has a kid, or parent, ever asked, "How will this learning apply to the curriculum standards?" We get that question a lot from educators, but never from kids or parents. They don't care about standards; they are excited to be free to learn about something THEY want to learn. Immediately kids start firing off project ideas, deciding on the spot that they have their project idea in mind and need everyone to get out of their way so that they can start. Well, we have to slow them down a bit at that point. We appreciate their enthusiasm but we have seen this behavior before and it normally does not end up very well.

Our process for the program is a bit slower than deciding a project idea on the spot and immediately getting to work on it. We know that kids this age are impulsive and move from one topic to another with the speed of light. It is our duty as their guides to slow them down and make them really delve into possible ideas, develop them, and see if they will really work.

Kids get a good half hour to talk to others, sketch out possible ideas, think, imagine, wonder, ponder and collaborate. More often than not, an idea that a student HAD to do ten minutes ago is now something else about which they are equally passionate. The change is that quick and that dramatic. That's the way things go in middle school classrooms. We encourage all of the talk, the false-starts, collaboration, sketching, writing, list-creating and other mechanisms for leveraging more ideas. We know that no one will come up with their real project idea during this time. We see this time as a way for kids to experience many first attempts at getting an idea. Their real ideas are still a couple of months off.

At the end of the day, at least half of the kids are dead-set on starting their "20% Time" project that night. They know what they are doing, are passionate about it and will have their project completed within the week. We sit back and smile, knowing that some teachers would pay good money for this kind of excitement in their classes. We also know that this excitement will come to a crashing halt once the kids realize that their initial ideas are not really the ones that have "legs". For any number of reasons, the project may not be a good fit for "20% Time". Normally, in the next couple of weeks, the kids will realize that they will hit a few dead ends along the way toward their real "20% Time" idea. And that is ok!

We watch the kids leave, not caring about tomorrow or next week or next month. This kind of enthusiasm for school is EXACTLY what we want to see from the kids. They finally get a chance to control their own learning, not just trudge through something the teacher puts in front of them with a due date lurking. No, each student will create their own project, figure out how best to learn, build, research, make or create the project, and then discover the best way to demonstrate their mastery of their learning project. We revel in this moment. "Yes!" we both yell at once, after the kids have cleared the halls.

Kick-Off Introduction and Notes

Today we begin "20% Time" projects. During this period, we will explain to you why we feel that these projects are essential to your learning this year and your development as a lifelong learner. We do not feel that traditional schools do a very good job at nurturing the ingenuity that is within each of you. Let's listen to Ken Robinson talk about that.

Video (TED Talk) - Sir Ken Robinson - Do Schools Kill Creativity?

Everyone is motivated by something different. Our "20% Time" program is designed to figure out what motivates you and make sure that your passion for learning is included in our classrooms this year. Let's check out Daniel Pink talk about motivation.

Video (TED Talk) - Daniel Pink - The Puzzle of Motivation

Talk about the Concept of "20% Time"

Allow 30 minutes for brainstorming and collaboration.

Before the end of the period, mention some of the immediate upcoming events and the regularly-scheduled "20% Time" class periods each week.

"20% Time" Student Guidelines

1. You will spend 20% of our class time, or every Thursday in science and every Monday in social studies, working on 20% Time.
2. Choose a project that is new to you and something you wouldn't normally do in another academic class. If you are stuck, do some research on other educational "20% Time" projects and take another look at what Google has done.
3. You must produce a product or achieve some sort of learning goal. We will not grade your actual project. We cannot penalize you for working towards, but not achieving, a personal goal or accomplishment. We will grade you on numbers 4, 5, 6 and 8 in addition to smaller assignments throughout the process.
4. Prepare for Pitch Day by creating a one-minute "commercial" for your idea and pitch your idea to the Pitch Committee.
5. Prepare for Idea Showcase. Choose an adult to be your official mentor. During Idea Showcase, you will talk with dozens of students and adults about your project. It is during this time that you will have a good chance of securing a mentor.
6. Reflect on the process each week on a personal learning blog.
7. If, at any moment, you feel lost, overwhelmed, or uninspired, you must meet with us.
8. At the end of the year, you will present your project and reflect on the process in a student TED Talk.
9. Failure is an option. Simply learning from your mistakes teaches you a lot.

The Bad Idea Wall

After introducing the idea of "20% Time", we give kids a few days to ruminate. Then we introduce them to the Bad Idea Wall. All year long, this blank bulletin board with "The Bad Idea Wall" at the top has been staring at the kids in Melissa's room. They had no idea what it was and often asked questions about it. All we would say is, "We'll tell you about that soon." Using a physical, tangible hook like this helps to build the excitement and expectation for the kids.

On Bad Idea Day kids are given scraps of paper. Melissa explains to them that they are to write down at least five project ideas that they have. She emphasizes that we are not concerned with what the ideas are, just that the kids post their ideas. The push here is to get as many ideas up on that wall as possible.

Inevitably, one daring student will scribble something down and pin it to the wall. As soon as one idea is up there, the rest of the kids begin writing down ideas. We encourage kids to look at the ideas that others are posting, tweaking those ideas or using them as a springboard to other ideas. We tell the kids that no idea is off the table. When kids ask why we would post bad ideas and not good ideas, we tell them that often the best ideas come from the initial bad ideas. There are bad ideas, we tell them, but good ideas can grow from them.

We stress that the ideas do NOT have to be school-related. This project does not have to be curricular. The kids can come up with ideas about anything that interests them. Most of the time, the things that interest them are not found in our regular seventh grade curriculum. When kids realize that their projects don't have to be "school-y" then their minds and ideas open up even more. There is a general sense of relief in the room and kids dare to dream bigger. What the kids, and many adults, don't see is that through these "20% Time" projects, many of the overarching learning goals are going to be satisfied.

Soon the room is buzzing with sharing, writing, and posting. Kids are having discussions about their ideas, sharing past experiences, and collaborating without even knowing it. Dozens of ideas hit the wall within the first five minutes and the kids are off and running. The first few minutes of priming the pump are essential because as some of the more outlandish ideas (time travel, etc) get out, the kids start concentrating on other ideas that they may actually want to turn into a project.

We pepper the kids with seemingly bad ideas during this stretch. "Fifty years ago, who would have thought that we could have a battery-powered phone that could go with you everywhere?" "Fifty years ago, who would have thought of the concept of e-mail?" There are many examples we use to show kids that some of the most outlandish ideas ever imagined have turned into our essential everyday items. These crazy ideas are not so crazy anymore.

Many times, the very traditional students crank out five ideas and say, "Okay, I'm done. What do we do now?" Well, we ask them to continue to crank out more ideas. "But you asked for five. I did my five. I'm done. What is next?" they say. The point of the exercise is to get the kids imagining and dreaming, not posting five ideas. We try to coach the kids to dig deeper and think of even more ideas.

The Bad Idea Factory is also an idea exchange. Kids look at what is posted and think, "Oh, I thought of doing something like that!" and they post more ideas. GPS Shoes for one student could become Sonar Shoes for the Blind, an actual project from our 2013-14 group. The initial "bad idea" was enough to spark the imagination of another student who ran with the idea.

For students, this kind of freedom takes some getting used to. Suddenly, the tables are turned on them and they are responsible for coming up with their own ideas, their own learning, and their own projects. It is liberating for some and scary for others. The day of sharing, fun, and laughter goes a long way toward giving kids confidence that they are all in this together and that maybe some of their crazy ideas are not really that crazy! Once they take off the self-imposed limitations, they can soar. The Bad Idea Factory helps them get rid of those limitations.

Brainstorming Guide - Day 1

"20% Time" Brainstorming Guide

1. List all of the things you've ever wanted to do, physically, and never been able to.
2. List all of the things you've ever wanted to do, mentally, and never been able to.
3. Think of some ways you might be able to help your community.
4. Think of some ways you might be able to help your school.
5. Think of some hobbies you've always wanted to try but never got around to figuring them out or learning more about them.

Now, choose your favorite three from above and free write on each of them for five minutes each.

Do this exercise on a separate sheet of paper and staple it to this handout. Use the questions below as a guide.

What would your goal be? How would you get there? Would you need any help? How can you work on this every week? What would your "20% Time" work look like in class?

Brainstorming Guide - Day 2

20% Time Brainstorming Guide

Researching - Be very specific in detail when answer the following questions.

My "20% Time" Project is going to be:

My final product/goal/accomplishment will be:

What do I need to know about my topic to be successful?

What will be easy about this project?

What will be difficult about this project?

Will most of this project be in class or outside of class?

If outside of class, what will I do during the class "20% Time"?

When you think you have your idea outlined completely, please make an appointment with Mrs. Hellwig or Mr. Eckert for approval to move forward. Once you have approval, you may begin working on your project.

Pitch Day

After our "20% Time" Kick-Off Day, we immediately begin planning Pitch Day. Pitch Day is one of the "Big 3" High Stakes Days of our "20% Time" program, and a time when kids can really focus on and crystallize their idea and learning processes. The pitch committee is made up of several district officials. We like to include these educators because we want them to see the genius that is in every child. We include our superintendent, assistant superintendent, building principal, assistant principals, curriculum coordinators and principals from other school buildings if they are available. Indeed, this is a high-stakes day for the kids and they give it the seriousness that it deserves. During the few weeks that precede Pitch Day, the kids begin fleshing out their project ideas. They will have a chance to present their ideas to a committee in order to receive feedback on both their ideas and processes of learning. It is a time when they concisely express their idea in order to "sell" the committee on the project. The feedback they receive from the committee ranges from advice on project ideas to appearance and presentation style. It is on this feedback and our own observations of the pitches that we assess the kids for Pitch Day.

Melissa and I allow about three weeks for the kids to prepare for Pitch Day. By this point, they have been given ample time to develop their ideas and do some preliminary research. The only thing that the kids need at this point is a viable idea and some sense of the direction where they would like to take the project. Many kids believe that they should have a significant part of the project finished but this is not the case. Pitch Day is really a time for kids to receive the green light to begin the project in earnest.

We plan for each project (be it individual or group) to have a five-minute Pitch Day presentation. During this time, they will "pitch" their idea, just like in the television show *Shark Tank*. The kids will try to sell to the committee that this is a worthy idea and learning process. In order to do this, the kids must have good command of their project ideas.

The five minute presentations are roughly divided into three sections: video, project description, and questions from the committee. We ask each individual or group to produce a one-minute video pitching the project and telling the committee what learning will occur and what product or program, if any, will be created. Essentially, the video is a commercial for the project. After the video, the kids talk about the project, describing what they intend to do and the learning they believe will occur. Lastly, the committee asks the kids questions both about the content of the project and the process of the project. This part of the presentation is crucial because often these questions help direct the kids in a way they had not thought of before or helps them focus on secondary learning that may take place.

Five-Minute Pitch Presentation

0:00 - 1:00	Student/Group shows one-minute video to committee
1:01 - 3:00	Student/Group discusses project goals and learning goals
3:01 - 5:00	Student/Group answers any questions from the committee

How many times have educators been an audience to kids who tell them what they will be studying for the next seven months? Probably not many. What normally happens in schools is that the the teacher tells the kids what they will be learning during the course of the year and how they will be learning it. Pitch Day is the opposite of traditional schooling and, quite frankly, kids are very nervous. For most of them, they have never been asked before what they want to learn. It is not their place to choose their own learning in schools. It is "given" to them; they have no stake in the learning. In our "20% Time" program, they are at the epicenter of their own learning.

A couple of days before Pitch Day, we coach the kids, telling them that no one knows more about their project than them. They cannot fail or be embarrassed during Pitch Day because, even though they have not completed the project yet, they are the experts in the room when talking about THEIR projects. We even ask our Chorus teacher, who has vast experience with stage presence, to work on some public speaking exercises with the kids as a group and meet with each of the kids individually to go over some finer points. Working with this teacher gives the kids a lot more confidence when they meet the committee. We also coach the kids on how to dress for success, walk into the room, introduce themselves to the committee members, and begin their presentations. We feel it is very important to make a good impression on the committee. Indeed, in our talks with committee members after Pitch Day concludes, it is evident that the kids have taken our advice to heart and the committee is impressed with the students.

The following is a sample schedule of our Pitch Day. For Melissa and me, most of the work has already been done. We have prepared the group lists with links to both the kids' videos and blogs. The videos are cued up and ready to go. This preparation helps save time and time is of the essence on Pitch Day. The only way we can stick to a schedule is to have everything ready to go for each group. We hold firm to the five minute limit on pitches. If we don't, the day will not work logistically.

Pitch Day Schedule:
At 8:15, the committee members show up. We separate them into two equal groups. One group (A) will see half of the presentations and the other group (B) will see the other half of the presentations. Each committee member has a stack of "feedback sheets" on which to take notes that the kids will see the next day. Feedback is important and we want the kids to have real feedback.

At 8:20, the morning bell rings and kids go to their lockers before moving to their first-hour classes.

At 8:35, our kids move to two empty classrooms that we have "borrowed" from other teachers. Here they will stay and work until it is their turn to present.

At 8:40, we begin calling up the first two projects for each room (Room A and Room B). The first student goes right in to begin while the second student stands outside the room "on-deck". When one presentation is over, the "on-deck" student goes inside the classroom and the student who just presented goes back to the holding rooms to notify the next student on the list that they are now "on-deck". See schedule examples below.

Pitch Group A

8:40 - 8:45	Publishing a Book
8:47 - 8:52	Project Peanut Butter
8:54 - 8:59	Stereotypes
9:01 - 9:06	Chocolate Panaffle

Pitch Group B

8:40 - 8:45	Parker's Swim Caps
8:47 - 8:52	PVXS Animation and Comics
8:54 - 8:59	Friendly Candy
9:01 - 9:06	She's a Fashionista

At 10:30, we have finally gotten through all of the project presentations. About 18-20 project presentations will have taken place in each of the rooms. Now it is time for the kids to go to their regular classes. Pitch Day is over and the kids can breathe a big sigh of relief.

When they are finished, they feel proud and accomplished. We try to reinforce to them that they have done something that even most adults find to be terrifying: public speaking. Pitch Day is not just any public speaking, but speaking to the highest-ranking officials in our school district. It puts kids on an even keel with those adults who have normally steered their education. When the kids find out that they know more about something that the superintendent, the confidence they gain is enormous. The committee members gain a deeper understanding and respect for our "20% Time" program, while the students benefit from having a completely objective third-party giving them honest and constructive feedback. Since we have let the kids chart their own course, it's wonderful to watch them learn and grow from this process and take the advice from our panel and further evolve their ideas. Our main role on this day is to make sure the students are supported and ready, but if you ask us, our favorite thing about Pitch Day is that we get to stand back and revel in the giant strides our kids are making by simply being able to pitch their ideas to strangers who are time and time again amazed by their individual genius.

Pitch Presentation Criteria

Checklist for Pitch Presentation

- ❑ Students greet panel and introduce themselves before beginning their presentation
- ❑ Clear topic
- ❑ Motivation for project
- ❑ Substance (Be prepared to speak beyond what you included in the video)
- ❑ What they hope to get out of their investigation (what is the application of this knowledge)
- ❑ Kind of mentor they are seeking
- ❑ Inquiry Question at the end
- ❑ Appearance (professional dress)
- ❑ Voice projection
- ❑ Good eye contact
- ❑ Addressing panel questions
- ❑ Appropriate body language

Blogging

A few years ago, I spoke to another teacher about blogging. He was insistent about the value of blogging but I had no idea why. I mean, who has time? The workload of a teacher can be crushing and blogging was "just another thing to do". I didn't see the value of blogging; I had, however, just discovered Twitter and was finding my way around this so-called "tweeting". After becoming immersed in Twitter, I saw that many, many teachers were also bloggers. They shared successes and failures of their classrooms, reflected on the "whys" of teaching, and shared resources with anyone who wanted them. Hmmmm, I thought to myself, that is useful. I began to understand all the buzz about blogging. It could not only be a snapshot of my classroom happenings for others to see, but also a way for me to sit back, gather my thoughts, and reflect on best practices. I decided to give it a go. Who says old dogs can't learn new and collaborative technology?

Since our school is a Google Apps for Education (GAFE) school, the natural choice for my blogging was Blogger. I started building the template for our Harmonized Learning blog and, after choosing the look and feel and adding useful gadgets, I showed Melissa. She liked some, didn't like some, and so we worked together to tweak it so that everything was easy to navigate and that the most useful information for students, parents and colleagues was prominently featured.

Our first post, "What is Harmonized Learning?" (http://goo.gl/5Gnr1l) talked about our vision for our "20% Time" program and also about the role of our blog. We did not imagine during that early stage what an essential part of the program our blog would become. Melissa and I posted our thoughts about the project goals, our students' reactions to "20% Time", notable projects and ideas, the nuts and bolts of instituting a "20% Time" program, and our reasons for transitioning to this type of learning. For us, it was important that our blog not only communicate what was happening in our classrooms, but also why it was happening. We told the story of the learning and invited others to join in on the conversation.

This type of transparency has proven valuable not only as a conduit for collaboration for Melissa and me, but also as a way to help parents, students, administrators, and other members of the educational community understand and buy into our "Harmonized Learning" environment. "20% Time" is innovative and unfamiliar and it can be a hard concept to understand, especially for students and parents who have only been exposed to a more traditional education. When we have talked about "20% Time", we have often gotten blank stares or shaking heads in response. It is one of those things you have to live in order to truly understand it. Students become fully immersed in it and quickly figure out the depth of "20% Time". Parents, however, do not live it and so it takes longer for them to understand and buy in. One of the hardest things for parents to let go of is the mentality that since traditional school "worked" for them, it should be good enough for their children. Our blog has been essential for helping the parents, community members, and even our school colleagues to gain a feel for what "20% Time" really means.

After we got our "Harmonized Learning" blog up and running, we felt it was necessary for each student to keep a blog as well. After all, if blogging is valid for our learning and reflection, it could also prove valid for student learning and reflection. We wanted the kids to share the stories of their individual journeys. We wanted to see the ongoing progress and evolution of their projects and read about what they are exploring and how they are learning. We wanted the kids to reflect on what they have done and what they planned to do next. Reflection is difficult even for many adults and it takes time to become comfortable with the idea. Students, especially middle school students, are not skilled at reflection and need practice to learn how to record their thoughts and express their ideas effectively. As with any new skill, we were determined to give our kids the time, space, and coaching necessary for them to master this concept. Blogging has since become one of the main components of our "20% Time" program.

When I introduce a new project, I like to show a variety of finished, or nearly finished, projects so that kids can see how far they can take something. Concerning blogging, I want them to see all that an online presence could do. After going over the basics of blogging together, we start to explore the various tools available. The kids really love some of the gadgets that Blogger offers. Some are essential, like a way for readers to follow by email, and others are up to the kids to choose, like the "Puppy of the Day" gadget (a very popular gadget for middle schoolers).

The thing that we like about Blogger is that a blog can be as simple or as complex as a person wants to make it. Some of our kids who have felt a bit overwhelmed design simple, clean, and basic blogs. There were no bells and whistles and it was enough for them to have a platform to share their learning. For others, Blogger became a project unto itself. There are seemingly endless permutations of templates, gadgets, and formats that kids can use. Many imported their own photos as the background of their blog. Some coded their own gadgets. Some used audio and video. The blog became an expressive outlet not only for the kids to tell the story of their learning but also to showcase their creativity.

Once the blogs are created, Melissa and I require one blog entry per week. We have the kids first use a Google Document to record their blog post so that we can proofread. Once they have the green light from us, they can then post the clean and final copy to their blog. After a month or so of this method, we start to loosen the reins and begin to give them the autonomy to post directly to their own blogs with the reminder that how they come across in their blogs is how the online community will view them.

Some kids take right to blogging. They share pictures of their progress, discuss not only what they were doing but also why they were doing it, and talk about what their short-term and long-term goals are. Some really tell the story of their learning. It is beautiful. Others struggle. We expect some kiddos to struggle because blogging is a learned skill and not something that comes naturally to students, especially students used to the traditional model of learning (teacher gives work, student completes work, student hands in work, teacher grades work - repeat until the end of the year). We ask kids what they think, what they are learning, what they plan to learn, and how they plan to learn it. Suddenly, students talk about their role in their learning, their decision-making, and their take on the project. After all, they are in charge of their learning and they must articulate the story of that learning.

Often we read blogs like, "We contacted the corporate headquarters. We sent an email today." That is the entire post. We have to draw out these kids quite a bit. We ask questions. Why did they send an e-mail? What were they hoping to accomplish? What did they need from the company? What was the story *behind* the action? Kids then begin fleshing out their blog posts to incorporate more of the *story* of their learning. After all, people not only want to know *what* kids are learning but also *why* they are learning it. They especially want to know because the student is the one creating the learning. Indeed, the blog is a peek into the mind of a middle schooler.

Each year when we kick off blogging with the kids, we move last year's project blogs to a static page on our "Harmonized Learning" blog. We keep the previous years' blogs easily accessible while highlighting the current batch of student blogs. This way, the kids can see how much work others have put into their projects before them and it inspires them to meet and surpass their previously held expectations of themselves. Another great motivator is that the kids can monitor how many page views they have and where in the world their blogs are being read. Trust me, nothing inspires a middle schooler more than having their ego bolstered knowing that they have "fans"! After one kid stumbles upon the "settings" button and figures out they can track not only hits to the blog, but where those hits are coming from, it's all over. Every kiddo in the room is now tracking blog hits. It is not uncommon for a student to shout out in the middle of class, "I had a hit from Uzbekistan!"

The kids discover the power of a real and authentic audience. When students and teachers from around the world look at their blogs and leave comments for the kids, the relevance of their learning and blogging hits home. These kids are no longer writing for just the teacher; they are writing for the world! All eyes are potentially on them and that raises the stakes in their minds. The autonomy and confidence that a worldwide audience gives them is powerful. Suddenly they see themselves as experts. This transformation is awesome to witness. It is what we, as teachers, want to see for all of our kiddos; and it is what all the kids want for themselves - world domination!

"20% Time" Blog Planning Sheet

Topic:

Title of Blog:

Subtitle of Blog: What your site is about in ten words or less

Post Requirements:

Post #1: Intro: origin of their idea

Post #2: What they hope to achieve

Subsequent posts: Weekly updates with research, reflections, news about their project

Other posts may be mandated by teachers as the project progresses

Points to consider as you blog:

- Drafts must be shared on Google Drive with Harmony teachers, or saved as drafts on Blogger, and get approved before they go live.
- What kinds of things inspired you online this week?
- Will this be a narrative, informational, or persuasive post?
- What will your post title be?

Atmosphere of Blog: What type of personality will come through on your blog? Serious

Commentator? Playful Individual Content? Informational Guru? Discuss what atmosphere you will strive for and why it is most appropriate for your site.

Advertising Your Content: After you post, how do you plan to let people know that you have new content?

Idea Showcase

Once Pitch Day is over, the kids have a few weeks to work until their next big "high-stakes" event, the Idea Showcase. The showcase is like an academic poster presentation where kids can show off their project progress not only to a few committee members, but to the entire school community as well. The kids use the time between Pitch Day and Idea Showcase to explore their proposals, solidify the direction of their projects, and start putting their ideas together in what we like to call a low-tech, high-touch format.

For Idea Showcase, kids are responsible for creating a science fair project display board that will go a long way toward attracting and giving information to passers-by. They will use text, graphics, photos and other visually stimulating material to build their board into the foundation of their presentation. These boards will be the jumping-off point for conversations that the kids will have with curious visitors. We build the hype leading up to Idea Showcase by sending out emails to parents, our fellow teachers, teachers in other district schools, administrators, school officials, and the community at large (grandparents, neighbors, etc.). This day is all about the kids demonstrating their expertise to a captive audience.

One morning in February, we take over the school cafeteria or library. Each student uses one table, sets up their project board and any other materials they have brought in to help explain their project, and sits at the table ready to discuss the idea with others. When the doors open for visitors to enter, dozens of students, parents, teachers and district staff walk the tables, browsing interesting ideas, engaging in conversations about the projects, and maybe even signing up to be a mentor.

Each student keeps a mentor sign-up sheet on the table in case an adult who visits has expertise in the area of the project. If so, we encourage the adult to mentor the student. Mentorship can take many forms. We have had parents participate with the kids, helping build go-karts. We have had adults help organize the kids, making sure that the project is executed on a logical timeline. We have had scientific experts match up with a particular project, e-mailing back and forth with the students and turning them on to resources that we didn't even know existed. Mentorship can take any form, but we require each student to have a mentor. The mentor can be lined up before Idea Showcase or after, but this day seems to align many students with the mentors they will work with throughout the semester.

Sometimes the mentor is the child's parent. While others may doubt the effectiveness of this partnership because they fear the parent will take over the project, we encourage it. In fact, we champion any activity where parents and children have the opportunity to spend time working together on a common project and strengthening their collaborative relationship. Indeed, we have had many parents and students say that the highlight of their year was the amount of quality time they got to spend with their family member working on their "20% Time" project. Mentors play a valuable role for the kids in any aspect of their lives, and "Harmonized Learning" is no different.

I previously mentioned that our Idea Showcase is a low-tech, high-touch event. I say this because we eschew any technology for this high-stakes day. We want this event to be high-touch, not high-tech. We push the kids to interact with the visitors and discuss their ideas with them face to face. We encourage the students to use their project boards as a reference point but remind them that it is important for them to be able to concisely verbalize their project goals and answer any questions that the visitors might have. The goal is not simply to have them read their posters; we hope to see them demonstrating their own mastery of their project. Conversing for many is a lost art and this is one opportunity for the kiddos to practice those conversational skills.

We consistently have a great turnout for this day. Many teachers from our building bring their classes down to look at the projects. The kids browse their peers' posters and check out the projects that appeal to them. At the same time, the teachers also interact with our kids. They ask them questions, offer advice, and encourage the kids to keep moving forward. Dozens of parents come into the showcase to look not only at their own child's project, but at the other projects as well. Teachers from other buildings, especially ones who are interested in implementing "20% Time" themselves, also come to the showcase. Even our Superintendent loves to stop in during this fun and exciting day!

The Idea Showcase is a big deal for us. We also try to make it a big deal in our district. Remember that I mentioned earlier our Superintendent's enthusiasm for the program? Our building and district administrators are incredibly supportive. They realize that education needs to be personalized for kids and they nurture every opportunity for teachers to do so. When teachers decide they want to try something new, like "20% Time", they are encouraged and celebrated. As educators, Melissa and I understand that this kind of change to the status quo is risky and in some ways unconventional, but knowing that our administration supports risk-taking in an attempt to enhance the educational experience makes things so much easier. They have told us before that in order for the teachers to expect kids to take chances, the administration must likewise support the teachers when they take on new endeavors. Both Melissa and I feel extremely fortunate to work in a place where so many understand that learning takes different forms.

Like Pitch Day, Idea Showcase is assessed. We will talk the about assessment later in the book, but in short, Melissa and I take turns rotating the events that we evaluate and counting the grades into our respective subjects. What this means is that one year, I may walk around and evaluate the kids' performances for Idea Showcase, while the next year Melissa will do so. This year, it was Melissa's turn to assess the Idea Showcase presentations. Our time in the cafeteria was supposed to run from 8:45-10:30 in the morning. Well, at about 10:15, our Superintendent came to see the showcase. I found Melissa at one of the project tables and told her that we had to keep the showcase open late because our Superintendent just arrived. She replied, "Oh my gosh, good! I'm only halfway done! Some of these projects are so interesting that I keep talking to the kids about them." We kept the showcase open until Melissa had finished assessing and our Superintendent had seen all of the projects.

When all of the people have gone, students walk proudly, project board in hand, back to our classrooms. Those who dressed up usually ask to go to the bathroom and change back into their regular school clothes (because they are in 7th grade and dress clothes cause an allergic reaction). We usually debrief about the showcase, pointing out things that went really well and some things we can improve on next time. The kids offer feedback about the process as well, talking about their own projects and those of their peers. We insist that the kids blog about their Idea Showcase experience. Usually by this point, the morning is over and kids move on to their elective classes.

This year Idea Showcase went according to plan. We had some great conversations with teachers from other buildings, administrators, and teachers and students from our own building. I had a memorable conversation with a parent who was talking about what she thought "20% Time" would be based on what little we told the parents at Open House during the second week of school. She said, "I didn't know what to expect. I thought it was just another school project. I get it now. Looking around this room and talking to the kids, I get it. This is an awesome experience!" We could not have said it better.

Sometimes it is hard to wrap your brain around "20% Time". It can be difficult to imagine how it will look because it is so vastly different from regular classroom activities. Even though it is a relatively new model of learning, we truly believe that it is qualitatively better learning because of the motivation and investment of the kids. Until you are immersed in "20% Time", you won't get the full understanding of its power. Attending events like Pitch Day, the Idea Showcase, and TED Talks will help you gain a better understanding of just how powerful "20% Time" can be for students.

Idea Showcase Visual Criteria

As one of the few graded assignments in the "20% Time" project, the pitch poster has definitive criteria and a predictable outcome, unlike your open-ended exploration. Be sure to use the checklist below for an outstanding display and to help communicate your project to others at the Idea Showcase which will be held in the cafeteria.

Idea Showcase Checklist

3-sided (science fair style) poster board

Project Title

Name

Audience / user base / client base for this project

What do you expect to learn from this project?

Projected product that will come from this research by the end of the school year

Projected expenses of the project and how they will be covered

Projected resources needed and where they will come from

Project timeline

Mentor being sought

Mentor Sign-Up Sheet

Interested in helping out with this project? Do you have some expertise on this subject? Please sign up to mentor this project if you can. The kids would really appreciate it. Mentorship can be in person, through email, or Skype/GHO. Thank you.

1. _____

2. _____

3. _____

4. _____

5. _____

Checkpoint Assignment 1

There is a long stretch of time between Idea Showcase and student TED Talks. During that stretch, we ask kids to complete two Checkpoint Assignments. Both of these assignments are formative rather than summative; they are not "high-stakes" events. What we are interested in is what progress has been made since the Idea Showcase. We read the blogs weekly so we have a decent idea about what is going on, but we want the kids to highlight the accomplishments they have made during the time since Idea Showcase. This checkpoint acts as a way for kids to keep their focus on the project progress. The following is the assignment that we give the kids.

Due March 27, 2015

- Identify 4 elements that you have completed on your 20% Time project since the Idea Showcase in February. (All blog posts count as "one" element). State where the evidence is.
- Identify at least 3 tasks you want to/need to complete to keep your project moving forward.
- Reflect upon the progress you've made by answering these questions/prompts
- Have you accomplished what you set out to do so far?
- Write about your successes and failures so far.
- Write about what you want to do in the next 3 weeks and if it is possible.
- Explain in depth what you need to do to accomplish those 3 tasks.

- Please create a stand-alone visual presentation (Google Presentation, Animoto, WeVideo, etc) that will show all who watch what you have accomplished and the direction in which your project is moving. Your presentation needs to be thorough enough that it needs no explanation from you in order for the viewer to understand and should answer all questions stated above.

This is a GRADED assignment based not on the presentation itself but the content.

Checkpoint Assignment 2

Like Checkpoint Assignment 1, this is another formative checkpoint that gives the kids an opportunity to talk about the progress they have made since Checkpoint Assignment 1. We have found that by giving kids too much time between assignments or events, they may lose focus and fall behind. By keeping checkpoints spaced out every few weeks or so, the kids stay focused on their projects and ensure that they are progressing. The following is our Checkpoint Assignment 2.

(April 25)

In this exercise, you will show evidence of your "20% Time" project progress. Answer the questions below by showing tangible work that you have completed toward your project.

1. Using Checkpoint 1 as a reference, show the work that you completed toward your short term goals. Please insert links, screenshots, photos or any other evidence of your work.
2. You have three weeks left before TED Talks. What work remains for you to complete in order to have an informative talk.
3. What work do you wish you would have done by now that you have not (for one reason or another)?

Student TED Talks

The culmination of a year of student-driven exploration and education in our "20% Time" program is the day of student TED Talks. For those of you who may not be familiar with this term, the "TED" in TED Talks stands for technology, education and design. These talks are given by various leaders in an array of professions and can be about anything. They are all over YouTube if you want to explore further just what TED Talks are and can be. All year, the kids have been working on their projects, motivated by their own passion for the learning that they chose and discovering things about their projects, and themselves, along the way. On a May morning every year, we take over the school auditorium for our TED Talks, and witnessing the growth and transformation of both the projects as well as the kiddos since Pitch Day is a sight to behold.

Starting in early April, we begin to make arrangements for our TED Talks. We talk to our awesome drama teacher about trading classrooms so that we can use the auditorium. We enlist our school technology guru to help us setup the audio and visual equipment that we will need to record all of the talks. One of the most important things that we do leading up to this final high-stakes day is send invitations out to all of our school's staff, the kiddos' parents, district officials, and the community at large. We want as many people as possible to witness these great learning exhibitions. Last year, we even broadcast the entire morning on Google Hangouts on Air and were featured in our local newspapers!

As we get closer to TED Talk day, the kids become a little more anxious. As seventh graders, we know that many of them love to be the center of attention; however, it is usually on their own terms, and to a much smaller audience-their friends! Even for most adults, the mere idea of public speaking inspires cold sweats and heart palpitations. These kids are going to be on stage in the auditorium, alone, in front of a crowd that normally includes up to 300 people, talking about their projects for five minutes or so. It may seem like we are expecting a lot of our students by requiring things like TED talks, but as with most challenges, when given the support and opportunity to succeed, these kids show that they are truly capable of amazing things.

A lot of preparation goes into creating the TED Talks. We start during "20% Time" class periods by outlining an easy format. The kids can use a visual of up to three slides or a rotating slideshow of photos. We stress to them that this is not a PowerPoint presentation where they will point to the card and babble. This is a talk! They will face the audience and speak to them. Many kids will take advantage of the opportunity to use visuals but some do not. Some like a slideshow that shows photos of a building process, community experience or experiment. Some turn off the projector and use only their words as their presentation.

There are a few things we ask each student to focus on during the TED Talks. We want them to tell the story of their projects. We want them to discuss the origination of their ideas, why they are important to them, what their goals were, what learning occurred along the way, and what they feel they accomplished. Now, as I mentioned before, we do stress to the kids that we are not asking for a final product from this project. If they have them, GREAT! We have had students start successful businesses, build a go-cart, and even retro-fit a golfcart to be 100% solar powered. Some kids' projects, however, are research-based and never get to the development stage. That is fine because we are interested in their learning, and learning doesn't always mean production. As long as they can tell the story of their learning and demonstrate the time and hard work they invested, they will have a successful TED Talk.

After the kids develop their outlines, we give them time in the auditorium after school to rehearse their talks. They take to the stage, deliver their talks, and get constructive feedback from the teachers and kids who are present. This environment is very supportive because at this stage all the faces are familiar and everyone knows that they will eventually have to take the stage themselves and deliver their own TED Talks. Some kids, of course, are total hams. They jump up on the stage and talk things out beautifully, seemingly born with a microphone in their hands. Many kids, though, are shy, unpolished speakers who would rather be anywhere else but here. With enough practice and a good outline, these kids can shine, too.

Many of our students want to write out their entire "talk" and read it to the audience. We do not allow that. We stress to the kids that we want a talk, not a reading. They may take an outline on stage, but they must interact with the audience. They cannot just read off of a paper. The outline is there to help them remember the points they want to make. Much of this process is ironed out during rehearsals. Many kids take advantage of the rehearsal time; some students do not. We make sure it is available, but we do not insist that kids come. The *onus* is on the students. They get to make their own decisions. Whether they come to rehearsal or not, they will take the stage on the morning of TED Talks.

A few days before the TED Talks, I prepare a Google Doc for our technology specialist. On the document, I have the names of the presenters in order. Next to each presenter is a link to the visual that they created, if they have one. When it is time for them to go on stage, the technology specialist clicks the appropriate link and the correct visual appears behind the student on stage. The student then gets a clicker to go through the few slides and we are off and running.

Most of our student TED Talks run between three and five minutes each. We ask that they not take more than five minutes because with fifty students to hear from it can be a long morning of listening. Fortunately, even though they must sit still, listening, for over three hours with only a few breaks, the kids' behavior this day is usually excellent. They spend their time thinking about either their own upcoming TED Talk, or watching their classmates to see how their presentations stacked up. They all want to be the best!

When one TED Talk is finished, we have our "on-deck" speaker ready to take the stage. When the "on-deck" student heads to the stage, the student next on the list heads to the "on-deck" seat. This system helps make the morning run smoothly and minimizes transition time between talks. Having sent out a schedule for the talks the day before, many parents come in during the estimated time of their child's talk. We try very hard to stick to that schedule.

After all of the preparation is done and the logistics figured out, we sit back and watch an amazing display of learning by our seventh graders. The array of topics never ceases to amaze us. Adults from the school and community are inspired by the kids' passion and realize that the students learned so much and so deeply because they were passionate about standing at the helm of their own education. Many of the kids continue their project during the summer and even into the next school year. We love this. We always tell the kids that this project, while culminating for seventh grade in a Ted Talk, could really have no end date. Their projects, if chosen wisely, can have the potential to turn into something that they want to pursue for years to come. TED Talks are the kids' way to demonstrate what makes them tick, what they love to learn, and what they plan to do with this learning. In addition to the content of their project, they also discover a great deal about themselves as scholars, innovators, entrepreneurs, designers, artists, engineers, philanthropists, and teachers. This project helps them learn the skills that they will need to be successful in any situation they will encounter, in school or out of school. After all, this project was a big step toward opening their eyes to see what real learning looks like.

TED Talk Prep Sheet

With "20% Time" Ted Talks occurring in the near future, it is time to prepare for them. Students will begin creating presentations for their Ted Talks. Looking back over the entire semester, they will start taking notes on the highlights and lowlights of their projects and emphasize what they have learned.

Things kids must consider when they are creating their presentations:

- The story behind the project? (What motivated the kiddo to choose this topic?)
- The problems they encountered along the way.
- The problem-solving that occurred to overcome the project problems.
- What kids learned during the course of the project.
- How the group functioned (if it was a group).
- Why the project succeeded or failed (this should make up a LOT of your presentation).

Students will share their notes with Eckert or Hellwig by April 18 (for a grade) and then begin constructing their presentations and rehearsing. Ted Talks will take place in mid May.

Grading, Learning Goals, and All That Jazz

Grades, Grades, Grades… When we talk to teachers about "20% Time", one of the hardest things for them to wrap their heads around is the grading piece. That is completely understandable and it's not their fault; for years education bureaucrats and administrators have been emphatic about the importance of grades and testing. Grades still play a major part in education and, as teachers, it is natural to wonder about how grades are assessed for "20% Time"..

Since "20% Time" is very non-traditional, the grading process must also be non-traditional, and that can seem daunting for many educators. After all, when we let go of the idea that we are chained to a content-driven, test-evaluated educational model, we can then focus on the learning process and not necessarily the learning product.. When we make this ideological shift, then effectively assessing what learning is taking place becomes appreciably easier.

It isn't just our fellow teachers that Melissa and I see struggling with this paradigm shift. Our students have been indoctrinated by the same system that causes teachers to balk at the idea of something that, when compared to traditional classroom models, seems pretty radical. Lecture, test, repeat; to this is what they have grown accustomed. Some of our conversations with kids go like this:

Student: How are you going to grade?
Me: We grade on what you learn during your "20% Time" project.
Student: What if we don't learn anything?

Me: How can that be? Even if you fail, you'll still learn something.
Student: Those kids last year made a go-kart. What if we don't make anything?
Me: Some kids last year didn't make anything and they did fine. You can build or create something, research something, or do any kind of project you want. It just has to be something that you want to do.
Student: Can I still pass if I don't make anything?
Me: Of course. We are only interested in your learning. If you can show us along the way what you're learning, then you're going to be fine.
Student: I'm not sure I get it.
Me: That's okay. You will. It's different than what you're used to. Why don't you just live it for a while and you'll come to understand it.

Inevitably, despite having conversations like the one above, we have dozens of kids every year who believe they have to produce a product in order to get a good grade. That is how they have been trained. We spend a lot of time during our seventh grade year untraining that behavior. Do kids have to demonstrate their learning? Of course they do. Is there a specific way that we want them to demonstrate that learning? Absolutely not. They can show their learning in any way that they choose. They also learn all of the skills necessary to design and execute their own learning.

Inevitably, there is someone who wants to know about the learning goals? At every professional development session we've given, at least one audience member asks this question, and it is a good one. Our response is that if we are focused on learning goals at the beginning of the project, then we've missed one of the key points of the project. As terrifying as this may sound, "20% Time" is best when planned backwards as far as learning goals are concerned. I can justify every learning goal for which I'm responsible, but I cannot do that until the end of the project. When I see the work that has gone into each kid's journey, I can identify the learning goals that were completed. The kids can meet and satisfy every learning goal that our district mandates without even knowing it, driven by their passion and desire to learn what they want.

At one of our professional development sessions that Melissa and I gave for our district, there was a conversation that really hit home for everyone in the room and still resonates with me to this day. One of our elementary school principals asked about learning goals. Melissa responded, "Dr. A., can you tell me the process by which blood travels through the four chambers of the heart?" After pausing and thinking for a few moments, he could not. She continued, "Don't you see? That's the point. In schools, we use content and content goals to gauge learning, but you're a building principal with a doctorate and you didn't know the content that my seventh graders are responsible for. Does that mean you're unsuccessful? Of course it doesn't. It just means that that area of learning has not been relevant to you. It's the same with "20% Time." It is imperative that teachers who run "20% Time" program divest themselves of the idea that the learning goals must drive the daily class sessions and look more at the long-range learning process. As difficult as it is at first, they have to trust that the kiddos will satisfy the learning goals, albeit through unconventional ways, if we let them.

Grading has always been a sticking point. Over the last few years, we've decided on some general grading guidelines. Our school is an 80/20 school, meaning that 80% of the kids' grades come from summative learning events (tests, projects, etc) and 20% of the grades come from formative learning events (worksheets, observations, discussions, etc). Together, Melissa and I have decided that the three big performance events that count for 80% summative grades are Pitch Day, the Idea Showcase, and Student TED Talks. Since these are the high-stakes performance events that we built into the program, it only made sense that these would be the summative grades. All of the other work for the project would fall into the formative category: blog posts, checkpoint assignments, observations, and conferences. The summative events would demonstrate all of the formative work that the kids have been doing during their work time. This system of grading works well. It allows us to focus on the learning processes and allows the kiddos the freedom to learn without everything being a high-stakes, heavily scripted learning event.

Melissa and I have evolved our grading system logistics. I have done 20% Time both in English class and social studies class, depending on the school year and the class schedule. Melissa has mostly stuck to science class for her "20% Time" session. Of the three high stakes days, I grade Pitch Day, Melissa grades Idea Showcase and we both grade Student TED Talks. There are several formative grades as well, the most prominent of which is the weekly blogging. Melissa and I alternate weeks grading the blog posts. Each Monday, we remind the kids about their weekly blog and who will be grading it that week.

English class is probably the easiest class to justify grades and learning goals for "20% Time". Let's face it, "20% Time" involves a lot of writing. We write weekly blog posts, learning plans, reflections, scripts and correspondences (both inside and outside of school). It is very easy for me to find the seventh grade writing and reading goals in each of the projects even if the project has nothing to do with reading or writing. For some projects, reading and writing are primary skills and for others they are secondary skills. Either way, all of the students satisfy the learning goals. I can then assess their mastery of these goals all year long. Instead of giving the kids the content, they create the content and I can assess the tasks based on the content that they created. The kids learn so much more in this type of environment because they are responsible for their learning.

Some of you may be wondering, with all of the content and other stuff for which teachers are held accountable, how do we find time to fit in anything else, least of all something like "20% Time"? This is another popular question that we get during each PD session we lead. Our answer is simple: there is no time for fluff. We use four days per week to teach the given curriculum. We NEVER say, "We don't have time for '20% Time' this week." That cannot happen. We condense the rest of the curriculum to fit into 80% of the week and we become very efficient with our time. "20% Time" is non-negotiable. We may change the day of the week that it occurs from time to time, usually because we have a day off of school, but Melissa and I ALWAYS have "20% Time" one class period per week. The kids must be able to count on a consistent work time and we feel that this is so important that we are willing to give up other things in order to give this program the time it deserves.

Inevitably, when talking about grades, we have to discuss the student who doesn't do anything at all. Yes, we've had a couple. It is very rare that we have students who squander the opportunity to learn about anything their hearts desire, but it does happen. When it does, we have to stop and ask ourselves, "Are these the same kids who don't do the traditional work either? The ones who don't do homework? The ones who don't do classwork? Is "20% Time" invalidated because kids who wouldn't work anyway may not participate?" The answer is "Absolutely NOT!" We will not compromise "20% Time" because one or two students may choose not to participate. If anything, we have a better chance of engaging a greater number of students simply because of what "20% Time" represents: a chance for them to buy-in to an education that they have chosen as being relevant to their own interests.

As a matter of fact, we have proven this. Over the past several years since implementing our program, we have consistently seen a higher rate of participation and completion with "20% Time" work than regular classroom assignments. I can think of only one student in the last two years that flat-out did not do a "20% Time" project. In fact, he did absolutely nothing. He moved from one idea to another, never really putting forth any effort. We coached him and worked with him but to no avail. However, even with factoring in that one student, ninety-nine percent of our students did "20% Time" projects, including all of our kids with IEPs and 504 Plans. This is part of what makes "20% Time" so wonderful and revolutionary; there are no limitations put on the students and the learning is tailored specifically to each individual's strengths, needs, and abilities.

Melissa and I are proof that teachers can satisfy the curricular learning goals through "20% Time" and accurately assess kids in such a way that they do not feel suffocated by grading pressures. Since "20% Time" can take any form in the classroom and be personalized for each individual student, kids will jump at the chance to participate. They become excited about their learning and take pride in the fact that they are now the ones calling the shots. They feel important and heard. They no longer feel powerless and little. They become fully invested not only in their project's success, but in themselves and their abilities. They see the relevance to their own lives and that relevance drives their passion. When we hook students and nurture them into lifelong learners, we have done them an incredible service. For Melissa and me, there is no greater sense of accomplishment. It is for these reasons that we so strongly believe in the philosophy behind "20% Time" and how it has helped us shape our own program, "Harmonized Learning", a program that we couldn't fathom teaching without.

Students Reflect

Each year, we have the kiddos reflect on their "20% Time" experiences. Because this project is different from anything they've ever experienced before, we usually expect the feedback to be all over the place. Well, we are not disappointed. The following are comments from students after they completed the projects, did their TED Talks, and had some time to reflect.

"I really liked this 20% Time project because we were able to choose something that we were interested in and I hope we can do something like this next year." - Kaiden

"When I was trying to use cheap molds and plastic sometimes it would have been easier to just quit rather than continuing and figuring out how to fix it. Once I did get past these hurdles I finally got some final product that I am happy with." - Steve

"The TED Talks were not something I was looking forward to. Even though I didn't want to do the TED Talk I thought it was good for me to get up and talk in front of people about something I am passionate about." - Fiona

"I liked 20% time. The fact that we could choose anything we wanted was awesome but was also complicated. There were so many possibilities that I was overwhelmed. That was also a good thing though. The fact that there were no limitations was good because we got to come up with things that we were really passionate about, and were really motivated to work on." - Lindsay

"I learned how to make a website, how to blog well, how to manage my time, and how to get a project that needed to do a lot at home done. This was a great learning experience and it should be used more in schools." - Jimmy

"I did not like the fact that we had to use a blog. I was not very good at keeping up with it and I often got behind on it. It was a good way to keep people updated but it was not something I was good at constantly doing." - Gretchen

"I think that this whole 20% project idea is a good idea for learning, it helps kids think more about the things they love to learn about." - Matthew

"If I had worked by myself, I would have come up with something in which I was more passionate and would not have had to rely on others to do their part. It was a good lesson learned. I realized that I am more comfortable relying on myself than others and that not everyone has the same level of determination as me." - Ben

"I thought it was very interesting and fun because I got to learn about whatever I wanted to. Of course in the end my idea didn't really work but it was nice to have my imagination run rather than make a project off of something you guys taught us or take a test over a subject." - Chris

"My 20% time was a pretty good project I think. What caused its downfall was me. I was too confident and arrogant and I think I've learned to not do that." - John

"Starting in December was difficult for most projects, especially clubs, because you are starting the middle of the semester. I felt that for some of our projects, we needed more time to get the project started." - Macy

"There were a lot of things we did great in. For example we learned a lot about music. There was one song where we had to conduct 12/8 time which means

there are twelve eighth notes per measure. We had never done this in class before so we had to learn it." - Lauren

"So I guess you could call that susailing, which isn't a real word but it means failing and succeeding at the same time, but it's something us Modern Music kids like to say." - Ella

"We went on youtube and found how to make a DYS (do it yourself) hovercraft. When we followed the instructions exactly the hovercraft didn't fly. And at that is when me, Alex, Spike, and parents decided that it was time for improvements." - Jonah

"I felt good about my own learning experience with this. I felt like I learned a lot. It was new and something I'd never had the chance to try before. I liked it. I liked the freedom to choose what I did during that time and I'm proud of what I did." - Alex

"For me, I have found that I want to continue helping others and work in social services when I'm older. Using 20% time for our project Pictures For Africa was also an amazing learning experience. I have learned that when you put your energy into something you are passionate about, you will achieve the goals you set for yourself." - Sydney

"Overall this has been an amazing learning experience. I have realized that if you put your mind to something and make time to do it you can achieve great things." - Grace

"I thought that the 20% Time Project was a good opportunity to challenge myself and to try to fulfill a dream I've had for a long long time. I think I may have contributed a little more to the project than my partner. Although he is a good person and fun to be around I do wish he had helped me more. I think my project succeeded and failed at the same time." - Conner

"When you and Mrs. Hellwig first started telling us about Twenty Percent Time Projects, honestly, I was super excited. Never in any grade had I been allowed to work on any project I desired." - Ethan

"I think we could've been more productive with our time in school than we were throughout the year. When the project was done and over with we had accomplished a full functional Go-Kart with an mp3 sound system." - Louis

"I didn't like this project is because I don't know how to work independently on my own without having some type of schedule or something to me keep on track. The next reason I didn't like this project is because I feel that it holds nothing that's worthy of learning. It takes time out of a regular school week to learn the important things in life that we will never use." - Toby

"It's no secret, this project didn't really work for me. With my inconsistency to stay with a project, I never actually got that much done. It put me through a lot of stress to have to constantly change projects, and I feel now that I will have more self discipline and motivation to get things done. I learned a lot from this project, even though I really didn't like it." - Andrew

"The TED Talk was stressful to say the least. First we were way ahead of schedule and my mom was freaking out and then the mike broke. That's not even including the stage fright and tech problems. But according to my mom I was, "Calm and collected." Maybe I'll go into poker if that's what I looked like." - Isaac

"I'm still debating whether I liked 20% time or not, it was........... interesting." - Jessica

For Further Reading

If you want to read further about motivation, creativity, "20% Time", Genius Hour, passion-driven learning, and other topics related to a progressive education in schools, the following list of titles is a good start.

Drive by Daniel Pink
Out of Our Minds: Learning to be Creative by Ken Robinson
Pure Genius by Don Wettrick
The Element: How Finding Your Passion Changes Everything by Ken Robinson
Readicide by Kelly Gallagher
A Whole New Mind by Daniel Pink
Teach Like a Pirate by Dave Burgess
Book Love by Penny Kittle

I also recommend engaging on Twitter. There are hundreds of weekly Twitter edchats that you can join anytime. The amount of democratic professional development available to teachers these days is astounding. The best thing you can do is put yourself out there and make connections. You never know what doors will open up for you. If you find yourself on Twitter, look me up (@dayankee).

Acknowledgements

There are many people who inspired me to write this book. The most obvious is my partner in crime, Melissa Hellwig. Together we have built a comprehensive, pure "20% Time" program that incorporates the kids' passions into their learning and into our classrooms. She is a tireless advocate for personalized learning and one of the elite teachers with whom I've had the privilege to work. Her ideas and work inspire me daily. She is a superstar.

One day, while talking to Matthew Park about all of our "20% Time" learning, he said, "Why don't you write a book? You obviously have a lot to share." After ruminating on the idea for a while, I decided to give it a whirl. He was my second pair of eyes on the book, suggesting things to emphasize and stories to tell. He also designed the book cover. Without him, this book would not have happened. I owe both Melissa and Matthew a great debt of gratitude for all of the inspiration and help that they provided.

I also want to recognize the kids. Without our students amazing us everyday, we would not have developed such a program. We were inspired because their learning was so dazzling. They showed us that if teachers give students room to create, innovate, research and invent, they will exceed any expectations that we had for them. Our students prove that all kids want to learn and build the skills necessary to become lifelong learners. It is an understatement to say that we have learned as much from them as they have from us.

www.ingramcontent.com/pod-product-compliance
Lightning Source LLC
LaVergne TN
LVHW052257070426
835507LV00036B/3300